OREGON
FAVORITES

Published by the Navillus Press
1958 Onyx Street
Eugene, Oregon 97403
www.oregonhiking.com   Printed in Korea

Cover: Mount Hood from Trillium Lake. Back: Phantom Ship in Crater Lake. Page 1: PCT
at North Sister. On this page: North and Middle Sisters from Tam Lake. Page 4: Clear Lake.
Page 5: Imnaha. Page 6: Goodman Creek.

SAFETY CONSIDERATIONS: The fact that a trip is included in this book, or that it may be
rated as easy, does not necessarily mean it will be safe or easy for you. The author has hiked
all of the featured trails. Nonetheless, construction, logging, and storm damage may cause
changes. Corrections and updates are welcome and are often rewarded. They may be entered
at *www.oregonhiking.com* or sent in care of the publisher.

OREGON FAVORITES

TRAILS AND TALES

WILLIAM L. SULLIVAN

NAVILLUS PRESS
EUGENE, OREGON

CONTENTS

INTRODUCTION

Many Oregonians are familiar with my guidebooks to the state's outdoors. More than a quarter million copies of Sullivan hiking guides are in print. But fewer people know I also write a newspaper column in Eugene. This book is a selection adapted and updated from my columns, telling my favorite stories and describing my favorite places.

Unlike my other books, this one is arranged by season. Some destinations really are best in spring when the widlflowers bloom. Others peak in fall when huckleberries ripen. To make it easy I've color-coded the headings for each month. Warm shades of orange identify summer trips. Cool blue tones mark winter adventures.

I hope you'll curl up in an armchair and read this book as you would any collection of stories. If you're inspired to try a trip yourself, pay special attention to the book's boxed inserts. This is where I've corralled the driving directions and other details. Keep in mind that some of the adventures described here can be difficult, exploring remote and dangerous country. Choose a trip that matches your abilities, tell someone where you

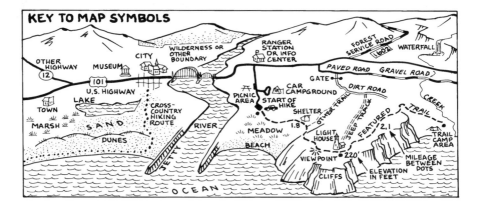

KEY TO MAP SYMBOLS

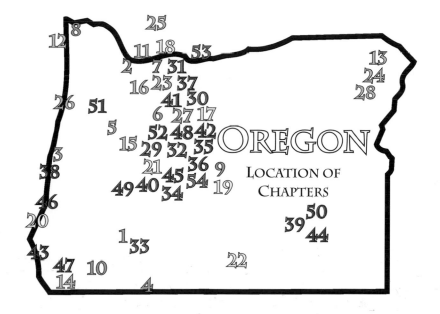

are going, and always take proper equipment—precautions that I describe in more detail in my outdoor guides.

A few of the columns here first appeared in *Eugene Weekly* between 1992 and 2000, but most are based on the "Oregon Trails" feature published monthly in the Eugene *Register-Guard* since then. I would like to thank both of these excellent newspapers, and their outstanding editors, for years of encouragement and support.

Surprisingly often, people ask me to name the "best" Oregon adventure. Oregon is such a diverse state, ranging from desert mountains to coastal rainforest, that it's hard to choose just one favorite spot. Likewise, our seasons bring such a variety of snow, rain, and sun that it's hard to choose a single best month. In this book I'm offering a spectrum of destinations and seasons to show the breadth of Oregon favorites.

William L. Sullivan
Eugene, Oregon

MARCH
IN OREGON

SKIING CRATER LAKE'S RIM

March means daffodils in the Willamette Valley, but at Crater Lake National Park, it's prime time for ski adventures.

Only a few snowshoers and Nordic skiers attempt the spectacular three-day ski tour around Crater Lake each year.

Most of these diehard adventurers are confronting a midlife crisis.

Well, at least some. After talking with several other Eugene skiers who were facing ominous, round-numbered birthdays, we resolved as a group to stop griping about our age. Instead we would do something about it. We would ski around Crater Lake.

The trek cannot be taken lightly. Once you set out around the unplowed, 33-mile Rim Drive , there are no shelters and no shortcuts back. Dizzying thousand-foot cliffs block all access to the lake itself. Cell phones rarely work here. Three areas along the route are prone to avalanches.

Of course you can also sample Crater Lake's spectacular winter views with a day trip. This is a wise warm-up before tackling the entire rim loop.

Rangers lead free one-mile snowshoe tours to the rim at 1pm every Saturday and Sunday from December through April. The park provides free snowhoes for the 90-minute walk. Participants have to be at least 8 years old, and pets

Left: Spring brings green to the canyon of Portland's Balch Creek.

Right and above: Spring is also the best season for snow trips at Crater Lake.

Wizard Island from Discovery Point.   *Below: Rim Drive near The Watchman.*

aren't allowed. The tours are limited to 30 people, so it's a good idea to reserve a spot by calling ahead at 541-594-3100.

For a day trip on your own, start by driving the plowed road up to Rim Village. Then ski or snowshoe clockwise along the lake's rim a mile and a half to Discovery Point.

This is the spot where John Hillman and a group of gold prospectors "discovered" the lake in 1853. To be sure, Indians had known about the lake for millennia, but they considered it such a dangerous and spiritual place that they hadn't told pioneer settlers about it.

These days, Rim Village has a cafe and gift shop that are open all winter. Crater Lake Lodge, however, is closed until mid-May. Unless you're prepared to snow camp, the only lodgings nearby are at the rustic Union

Creek Resort, 20 miles west toward Medford on Highway 62. In snowy woods near the Rogue River, this old-timey hostelry offers a tiny general store, nine rooms, and 23 cabins.

If you're serious about tackling the 33-mile ski trip around the rim, rangers suggest going in March or early April. By then the worst winter storms have passed and the days are longer.

In winter, tenting is allowed even on Rim Drive near Cleetwood Cove. In summer, camping is banned within a mile of the rim.   Below: Applegate Peak from Sun Notch.

Heeding that advice, our midlife crisis support team drove to Crater Lake in March. Two miles before Rim Village we stopped at the Steel Visitor Information Center for our free, mandatory backcountry overnight permit.

You're required to pick up a backcountry permit in person. That gives the rangers a chance to read you a long and frightening list of winter warnings. Avalanches may be rare in Oregon's Cascade Range, but Crater Lake gets a staggering 44 feet of snowfall, so the risk is real.

Before letting us go the ranger checked that we'd brought avalanche beacons, probe poles, and snow shovels. We'd be ready to dig out anyone who happened to get buried along the way.

Finally we drove up to Rim Village, where six-foot snowbanks surround the parking lot like walls. When we climbed up the wall the lake gaped before us, as astonishing as an ocean lost in the mountains.

We set off, staggering under the weight of 50-pound backpacks. After nine miles, the tracks we had been following suddenly ended. The previous skiers must have turned back.

We pressed on, breaking trail through deep snow. The farther we went, the more arduous this task seemed. We might as well have been wading uphill through wet cement.

11

Finally, as stars began to twinkle over the lake's dark eye, we set up our tents on a bare patch of pavement in the middle of the road. Then we collapsed into our sleeping bags, exhausted.

The next morning we were feeling cocky about our progress—not bad for middle-aged guys—when a wiry, white-haired gentleman with a tiny day pack skied up the road. He looked to be at least 70 years old. We hailed him, assuming he must have camped behind us.

The man shook his head. "No, no. Not camping at all. I left the Rim Village at 5:30 this morning. At my pace I'll make it around the lake by mid-afternoon." He tipped his beret and glided breezily onward.

We were still staring after him when an elderly woman approached. "Did my husband come through here?" she asked.

All that day we followed this pair's tracks, in awe. Long herringbone-shaped marks proved they had skated up hills using a high-speed skiing technique that demands Olympian stamina. Where the sun had melted gaps in downhill slopes they had skied across pumice rather than stop to walk.

Unwilling to attempt the 33-mile loop in a single day, we took heavy packs with camp gear.

Trudging behind these superhuman seniors, we felt very young indeed. And for a while I wished we too had left our heavy packs behind.

But I changed my mind the second night. A huge moon lit the snowy forests with an eerie, false dawn. We'd briefly left our camp for a quick midnight jaunt when a skier wearily approached on the trail. He was hardly twenty years old, with a thin jacket and a limp day pack. He wore downhill skis, rigged temporarily for Nordic travel.

He explained that he was a German exchange student at Oregon State University. Familiar with skiing from village to village in the Alps, he had decided to take a quick tour around Crater Lake.

Sunset from our last day's snow camp.

Now he felt as if the wilderness had swallowed him whole. All day he had seen no other skiers and no trace of civilization. He was out of food. His feet were blistered. Each step in his stiff alpine boots had become an agony. Nothing he had seen in the Alps had prepared him for the scale of Oregon's backcountry.

"How much farther is it to my car?" he asked.

"About six hours," I told him. "You'd better stay with us."

The young German student cut me short with a shake of his head. "No. I'm not stopping now." And he skied grimly on, tracing the moonlit rim above the starry lake.

The next day we saw from his tracks that he had cut across avalanche-prone slopes in the dark. He'd been lucky his immaturity hadn't cost him his life.

"Perhaps middle age is not so bad after all," I mused, unlacing my ski boots when we reached the van.

One of the others asked, "Then you're ready for the surprise party with black balloons and gag gifts of Depends?"

I sighed. "Let's talk about where we'll ski next year."

PORTLAND'S AERIAL TRAM

Portland's futuristic $57 million aerial tram has been compared to Seattle's Space Needle.

But wait a minute—at the top of Seattle's tourist attraction you get a revolving restaurant. At the top of Portland's tram all you get is a hospital.

Ah, but there's more for hikers. If you're game for a 4.4-mile walk you can complete a woodsy loop to Council Crest, a historic viewpoint atop Portland's highest point. This scenic circuit is known as the Four T's, because it uses a trail, tram, trolley, and train. If you do it right, you can even ride the tram for free.

The aerial tram is free downhill, so hikers often include it in a scenic loop.

It's a great excursion for a Saturday, when the tram runs 9am to 5pm. Weekdays the tram runs 5:30am to 9:30pm. The tram sits idle on Sundays, except for summer afternoons.

The best starting place for the Four T's tour is the MAX light rail station in Washington Park. If you're driving, you'll find large, free parking lots for the Oregon Zoo nearby.

Walk across the street from the MAX station to the World Forestry Building and follow the sidewalk a few feet uphill. Just before the entrance to the Vietnam Veterans Memorial, turn left on an unmarked gravel path into the woods. Behind the World Forestry Building you

turn left on the Marquam Trail, which crosses Highway 26 and climbs toward Council Crest.

The forest here is a mix of cedars, bigleaf maples, and vine maples, with an understory of frilly lady ferns, stern sword ferns, and delicate fringecup. Big white trilliums bloom best around April Fools Day, but that's also a season when you can expect a few patches of mud, so boots are better than sneakers.

The route up to Council Crest briefly follows a few streets (see "Hiking Tips" on page 16). At the high point of the Marquam Trail you'll have to detour across a lawn 100 yards to find the brick observation patio on Council Crest's summit, where plaques identify sights from Mt. Rainier to Mt. Jefferson. Even in less-than-perfect weather, views still extend from Beaverton to the Fremont Bridge.

Council Crest was named in 1898 by a gathering of church council picnickers. In 1906 the hilltop was converted to an amusement park, complete with roller coaster, observation tower, and landlocked riverboat. Until 1950 an electric streetcar brought excursionists up from the city in style. The carnival closed in 1929, however, and a huge water tank was built here in 1942. But dreamers and picnickers still love this grassy crest.

After soaking in the view, continue downhill on the Marquam Trail, crossing three city streets in a mile. This steep, wooded canyon was originally saved from development because of the unstable geology that makes

The tram ride includes first-rate views of downtown Portland.

Portland's west hills such a tricky place to build.

Although Ice Age glaciers never reached Portland, their outwash plains repeatedly filled the flatlands with dusty silt. During arid interglacial periods, huge dust storms blew silt onto the hills, leaving a layer of slippery topsoil up to 30 feet thick. Prolonged rains can launch landslides, especially where this layer is disturbed by houses or roads. Despite the danger, 200 apartments were proposed for this canyon in 1968. But volunteers raised over $1 million in a citywide campaign and saved the land as Marquam Nature Park.

The viewpoint patio atop Council Crest.

When you reach the hospital, catch a free ride downhill on the aerial tram. The Swiss-made gondolas complete the 3-minute trip at 22 miles per hour, jiggling

Getting There: Begin at the Washington Park MAX station next to the Oregon Zoo. If you're driving, take Highway 26 from downtown Portland toward Beaverton, pull off at the zoo exit, and park in the free lots at the MAX station by the World Forestry Center.

Hiking Tips: Walk behind the World Forestry Center, turn left on the Marquam Trail, and follow it down beside the Children's Museum to a paved street. Cross Highway 26 on a freeway bridge, walk left 150 feet along an on-ramp, and take the Marquam Trail up into woods to the right.

When the path ends at Patton Road, turn right on the sidewalk 200 feet and then turn left on Talbot Road for two blocks to find a wide paved path up into the woods. After 200 feet go up steps to the left on the Marquam Trail.

At the next junction, in 0.2 mile, the Marquam Trail dives down to the left, but first detour up across a lawn to Council Crest's summit patio. Then continue downhill on the Marquam Trail, crossing three city streets in a mile. Keep right at the first two trail junctions, following "Terwilliger Trail" pointers to SW Gibbs. Turn left on this street, walk downhill 7 blocks, continue under two pedestrian overpasses, and go straight up a covered stairway into the hospital to find the upper tram station.

The ride down is free, but then you'll need to buy a ticket to take the Portland Streetcar to Morrison Street, where you can catch a MAX train back to the zoo at Washington Park.

The Marquam Trail connects Washington Park with Council Crest and the tram.

stomachs as the car whoops past a central support pillar. The 78-passenger gondolas depart every 5 minutes. Views en route extend past the highrise condos of the South Waterfront District to Mt. Hood.

At the bottom of the tram line, catch a Portland Streetcar to downtown. Then use your streetcar ticket for a ride on a MAX train toward Hillsboro. Hop out at Washington Park to complete the Four T's, a loop that shows off some of Portland's prettiest parkland and best public transportation.

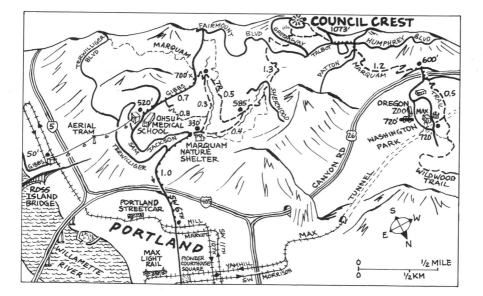

SWEET CREEK FALLS

The inner gorge of this cascading Coast Range creek is so narrow that the trail includes metal catwalks bolted to the cliffs. The star attraction is 20-foot-tall Sweet Creek Falls, but the path through this canyon's jungly rainforest passes a dozen smaller falls just as sweet. From late March to early May the walk is also awash with woodland wildflowers, including big, three-petaled trilliums and a rare local variety of pink fawn lily.

The Zarah T. Sweet family of Pennsylvania settled the sleepy valley here in 1879. The Sweets had gone west on the Oregon Trail in search of the perfect farm, and they kept on going west until they ended up here,

Trilliums (above) bloom in spring along this Coast Range path, which passes Ledge Falls (below) on its way to 20-foot Sweet Creek Falls (opposite page).

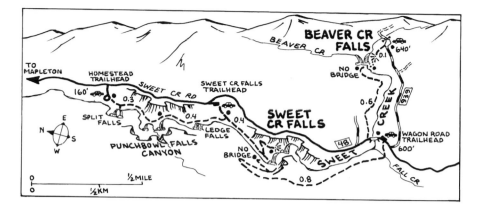

almost at the ocean. Portions of their early wagon road have been incorporated in the modern trail. Four trailheads along the route make it easy to hike the path in segments.

From the Homestead Trailhead a graveled path heads upstream past the first cascade, a split, 10-foot waterfall. Later, the trail hugs a cliff through a canyon full of punchbowl-shaped falls. Four-foot-thick Douglas fir trees tower above the creekside alder and bigleaf maple. Black, robin-sized water ouzels fly just above the creek's surface before plopping underwater to prowl the creek bottom for insect larvae.

After 0.7 mile a path from a second trailhead joins on the left. Continue upstream 0.4 mile to a cliff-edged plunge pool at the base of Sweet Creek Falls. A spur trail switchbacks up 150 yards to a viewpoint of an upper falls in a thundering slot, your turnaround point for an easy 2.2-mile hike.

Getting There: From Eugene, drive Highway 126 west 46 miles. Immediately before the Siuslaw River Bridge to Mapleton (15 miles east of Florence), turn left on paved Sweet Creek Road for 10.2 miles. Then take a paved turnoff to the right to the Homestead Trailhead turnaround.

Hiking Tips: Follow the trail 1.1 miles upstream to Sweet Creek Falls, and return as you came. For a longer hike, drive 1.3 miles up Sweet Creek Road to the Wagon Road Trailhead and hike 0.6 mile upstream to Beaver Creek Falls.

While You're in the Area: Swing through Mapleton to visit Alpha Bit, a charmingly funky commune-owned coffeeshop.

THE MODOCS' STRONGHOLD

The Modocs' story is an Oregon story, although the lava beds and tule lakes of their homeland lie just south of the border in California. For more than a century this tribe was forced to live in Oregon. Their borderland rebellion is the stuff of legend.

For five months in 1872-73, a defiant band of 52 Modoc men held off over a thousand US Army troops by using the lava formations of their ancestral grounds as a natural fortress.

Today, short hiking trails in the Lava Beds National Monument tour the geologic and historic sites of this often-overlooked corner of Northern California.

If you happen to be driving to Reno on other business, the area makes a nice halfway stop, with the only campground for miles. Even if you're not a gambler, the national monument here is still a safe bet for an uncrowded getaway to a land of crisp spring air and starry nights.

Even those who only have time for a quick trip can still hike the 0.7-mile loop to Captain Jack's Stronghold and explore the visitor center's Mushpot Cave. If you're not in such a hurry, spend the night at the national monument campground and hike three slightly longer trails.

May brings mules ears (below) to the desert near the lava fortress at Black Crater (above).

Start at the parking pullout for Captain Jack's Stronghold. The interpretive trail that begins here winds through a lava moonscape where pressure ridges, outcrops, and caves served as a natural fortress for Keintpoos ("Captain Jack") and his band of Modoc warriors.

The Modocs had been forced to leave their homeland here in 1864 to join the Klamaths on an Oregon reservation. Although the Modocs and Klamaths spoke similar dialects of the same language, they had long been blood enemies and did not want to live together. After more than 600 of the Modocs returned, the US Army arrived in November, 1872 to take them to the reservation by force.

Keintpoos stymied the troops and killed General Canby in a parley—the first US general to die in an Indian war. After Keintpoos' surrender on June 1, 1873, he and three other Modoc leaders were hanged at Fort Klamath, Oregon.

The remainder of the Modoc tribe moved to the Klamath Reservation after all, where they settled the remote headwaters of the Sprague River Valley, as far from the Klamath tribespeople as possible. To this day the villages of Beatty and Bly are peopled primarily by descendants of the Modocs.

After walking half a mile on the trail through Captain Jack's Stronghold, you'll reach a T-shaped trail junction. Turn right to complete a short loop back to your car, or turn left for a longer loop tour.

After this first hike, drive onward another 12.9 paved miles to the visitor center at the park's headquarters. Park here to tour the center's indoor displays. Then look for the entrance to Mushpot Cave, a railed pit with a steel

Each lava tube cave can take hours to explore. Confusingly, some have two entrances.

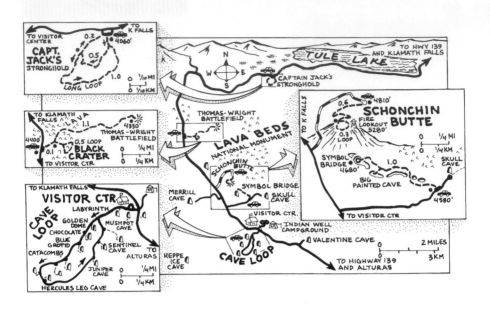

staircase in the middle of the parking lot.

Mushpot Cave is the only lava tube in the national monument that's lighted inside. The lights go off at 5pm in winter and 6pm in summer.

The 400-foot-long cave features "lavacicles" (where superheated gas remelted the rock walls), "cauliflower lava" (a chunky lava flow that puddled up on the floor), and a "mushpot," where liquid rock bubbled up from a lower cave.

Like all lava tubes, Mushpot Cave formed when a liquid basalt lava flow formed a crust but the hotter lava underneath kept on flowing, draining tube-shaped caves.

If Mushpot Cave catches your fancy, you can explore two dozen other lava tubes nearby. Simply drive the 1.3-mile paved loop road from the visitor center and stop at one of the many parking pullouts.

For these less developed caverns you'll need to remember some safety rules. Bring battery-powered flashlights (available at the visitor center). Never explore alone. Wear warm coats because the caves are cold even on hot days. Wear a helmet because many caves have low ceilings. Note that fires and gas lanterns are banned.

If you're staying overnight, head for the Indian Well Campground across the road from the visitor center. On your second day, consider hiking three other interesting trails. For the first of these recommended hikes, drive

The fire lookout on Schonchin Butte.

1.6 miles north from the visitor center toward Klamath Falls. At a sign for Skull Cave, turn right for a mile to a pullout on the left for Symbol Bridge. This 1-mile path follows a partly collapsed lava tube to a natural arch with prehistoric petroglyphs.

Larkspur on Schonchin Butte.

For the next hike, return to the main road, drive another 0.7 mile north, and turn right toward Schonchin Butte for a mile to road's end. From here a trail climbs 0.6 mile up the cinder cone to its crater rim. A 0.3-mile loop around the rim visits a fire lookout tower (staffed in summer) with a view from Mt. Shasta to Mt. McLoughlin.

For the final recommended hike, return to the main road and drive another 2.5 miles north to the Black Crater parking pullout. This path sets off across a sagebrush prairie with penstemon, larkspur, and other wildflowers in May and June. After 150 yards, fork to the right for a half-mile loop tour of Black Crater, a giant spatter cone with contorted, red-and-black gargoyle-like lava outcroppings along its walls.

Then return to the main trail and hike another 1.1 mile to trail's end at an overlook of the Thomas-Wright battlefield, where Captain Jack's warriors wiped out most of a 64-man Army patrol on April 26, 1873.

Ironically, the Modocs were not ordered to leave this land because it was wanted by settlers or farmers. At that time, the government's policy was simply to round up all the tribes in an area and put them on one reservation — in this case, the Klamath Reservation.

The forbidding lava terrain that the Modocs fought so hard to keep has hardly changed in the past 130 years. It remains as a monument not only to the high desert's stark beauty, but also to the spirit of people who were willing to fight for their homeland.

Getting There: To drive here from Klamath Falls, follow signs for Reno. You'll end up on Highway 39, which turns into Highway 139 at the California border. Turn right 8.3 miles beyond the border and follow signs for the Lava Beds headquarters. After 11.4 miles, park in a large pullout on the left for Captain Jack's Stronghold.

Hiking Tips: Note that pets are banned on trails.

Season: Although the trails are open all year, avoid the freezing winds of mid-winter and the blazing heat of mid-summer.

O ne of Oregon's newer state parks preserves a historic water-powered flour mill in the heart of the Willamette Valley.

Thompson's Mills State Heritage Site isn't far from Interstate 5, but surprisingly few travelers have left the freeway to explore this 21-acre pioneer relic.

Trust me, this is a great place to stretch your legs when you're driving that tedious straight section of Interstate 5 from Albany to Eugene. Bring binoculars if you're a bird watcher. Bald eagles often hang out along the Calapooia River here in March.

Kees and Margriet Ruurs spearheaded this particular park's renovation. When Kees was a child growing up in Dordrecht, Holland, he knew he wanted to be a park ranger. But Dutch universities didn't offer parks management programs. So he came to Eugene, completing a graduate program at the University of Oregon in 1974.

The Ruurs are adventurous folks. After college, Kees and Margriet

Kees Ruurs watches the mill's spillway. Above, the mill's mansion before renovation.

spent a decade in the Yukon. Then Kees walked the entire width of Spain.

Margriet has become a celebrated author of more than 20 children's books. Two of her titles, "In My Backyard" and "Wake Up, Henry Rooster!" may have been inspired by her move to rural Oregon.

In 2003 Kees accepted a job as manager for the Oregon State Parks' southern Willamette region, overseeing 60 parks within about 60 miles of his headquarters in Lowell.

The position was supposed to include a ranger's house where he and Margriet could live. No suitable house was available at the time, but the state had just bought Thompson's Mill. That property included a derelict 1904 Queen Anne mansion.

Sight unseen, Margriet suggested they move into the mansion.

Kees took pictures of the place to discourage her. Blackberry vines were growing through the windows. Piles of dead bugs littered the windowsills. Water damage and peeling wallpaper were everywhere.

"It looked like a Halloween haunted house," Kees said. "I told her we can't live there."

Margriet replied that they'd fix it up somehow.

And so, while state crews set about restoring the old mill, the Ruurs went to work on the scary mansion next door.

The mill's flour sacks served as wallcoverings.

The Ruurs tore out false ceilings, revealing that the rooms were actually 12 feet tall. They found the original interior doors and window moldings stacked in an outside shed, had them refinished, and reinstalled them.

They stripped the walls. In the process they discovered that the original wall covering had been linen flour sacks from the mill, complete with the mill's "Valley Rose" brand name.

The scariest thing they replaced was the house's dangerous 1904 wiring. Because the mill next door generated electricity, the mansion may have been the first rural home in Oregon to be wired.

For the first two winters that the Ruurs worked and lived in the house, the only heat came from a wood range in the kitchen.

The renovated house is open only by appointment, but the mill itself is ready for visitors.

The flour mill dates to 1858, one year before Oregon became a state. At that time wheat was Oregon's major export. Flour mills were in demand. Although the first building soon burned, it was rebuilt in 1862.

A scale model inside the mill shows the building's framework. Massive 40-foot beams for the structure were hand-hewn from logs with a broadax. Don't expect nails here—the beams are joined by mortises, tenons, and wooden pegs.

Once the mill was built, entrepreneurs platted the optimistically-named city of Boston nearby. The city's 88 lots were arranged around a town square in correct New England fashion.

Houses, stores, and a blacksmith shop soon opened in the little boomtown of Boston along the Calapooia River.

But then the Oregon & California Railroad came through in 1871, missing the town by a mile and a half. All of the town's buildings, except the mill itself, were jacked up and moved west to the railroad. Many still remain there in the town of Shedd.

The water-powered mill faced some engineering challenges. The power source is a sluggish creek in a flat valley bottom. By damming the creek a mile upstream and diverting the water through a canal, the mill builders managed to bring the water to the mill's headgates with a 16-foot drop.

With the four floodgates wide open, 1600 cubic feet per second of water roar through, filling the spillway twenty feet wide and ten feet deep.

Kees adjusts the floodgates that power the flour mill machinery.

Turbines inside the mill turn flywheels that move leather belts, powering all of the mill's machinery.

In the old days, wagons arriving at the mill would dump wheat in a bin. Elevators and augurs powered by the mill's belts would hoist the grain upstairs to one of 70 storage compartments. From there the grain would be funneled through chutes to the milling equipment. The original granite millstones, bought from France in 1858, are still on display.

The four silos beside the mill were the first built from concrete in Oregon. They date to 1917, when World War I increased demand for flour so much that the mill operated around the clock.

A short walkway separates the mansion from the mill.

From World War II until 1987, the mill turned out animal feed. From 1986 to 2005, the turbines produced electricity.

Oregon State Parks bought the property in 2003 for $856,000, using Oregon State Lottery funds. Another $1,350,000 went toward installing interpretive signs, painting walls, making the building safe, and providing wheelchair access.

The park includes a stretch of the Calapooia River and a one-mile millrace open to canoes. Work on the millrace and dam have improved passage for fish.

There are no plans to add campsites or trails to the park, according to Kees, because "it wouldn't fit in with the neighbors."

He and Margriet have since moved on to manage and develop other parks, but they always give special consideration to the neighborhood. After all, they don't just manage parks.

They live in them.

Getting There: From Albany, drive Interstate 5 south 5 miles to Exit 228, head west toward Corvallis 2 miles, and turn left on Highway 99E for 7 miles. Just before Shedd, turn left on Boston Mill Road for 1.5 miles to the Thompson's Mills parking lot on your left. The mill is open 9am-4pm, but can close during storms or floods. For information call 541-491-3611.

If you're coming from Eugene, take Interstate 5 north 22 miles to Halsey exit 228, drive left 2 miles to Halsey, and turn right on Highway 99E for 5 miles to the village of Shedd. At the far side of town, turn right on Boston Mill Road for 1.5 miles.

THE BEWILDERING BERLEY LAKES

I've struggled for years, and once I nearly died, attempting to find the Berley Lakes.

A glance at the Mt. Jefferson Wilderness map shows that this pair of lakes should be among the state's most popular destinations, winter and summer. The lakes are just 3 miles from a Sno-Park atop busy Santiam Pass. The nearly level route to the lakes follows the Pacific Crest Trail, perhaps the best known path on the planet.

So why are the Berley Lakes so rarely visited?

Part of the problem is that the Pacific Crest Trail misses the lakes by 200 yards. The unmarked connecting path plunges through a thicket to

A 2003 wildfire made it easier to see landmarks at Santiam Pass, but it's still confusing.

a hidden valley with a surprising view of Three Fingered Jack.

But that's only part of the problem. The Berley Lakes seem to be lost in a topographical vortex of confusion. Those who venture near risk bewilderment.

Eight times I have tried to ski or hike to the Berley Lakes. I have found the lakes only five times, even when using a global positioning system (GPS) device. These odds may not sound too bad, but they're actually terrible for a guy who writes guidebooks for a living.

For 14 years I featured the Berley Lakes in my hiking guide for the Central Oregon Cascades. After fielding emails from hikers who failed to find the lakes, and after a 2003 wildfire burned the first 2.5 miles of forest along the route, I finally decided to rel-

Three Fingered Jack in winter.

egate the Berley Lakes to the back of the book—an appendix of "100 More Hikes" where I stow faint, dull, or fragile trails.

This is an unsatisfying choice because the route to the Berley Lakes is neither faint, nor dull, nor fragile. It's just hexed.

Forget for a minute the times I've led groups to the lakes' hidden valley only to discover a valley with no lakes (possibly too far west?) or a cliff with no valley at all (perhaps too far east?).

Consider instead the overnight cross-country ski trip I took one March, when I actually found the lakes, but wished I hadn't tried.

Two ski buddies and I had chosen the Berley Lakes for a weekend snow camping trek because the route really is pretty level, and it's only 3 miles. We divided up the gear into three 55-pound backpacks. Our survival equipment included backpacking stoves, thick down sleeping bags, and a winter tent sturdy enough to withstand hurricanes.

The forecast was for a blizzard, which we took to be good news. It's always more fun to ski in a snowstorm than a rainstorm. Besides, we were prepared for winter weather.

I've never seen it snow quite so hard at Santiam Pass. When we stopped skiing for a quick lunch break, our tracks filled up behind us. At that point I realized we couldn't rely on the usual bail-out technique of heading back to the car by retracing our tracks.

We slogged onward through the deepening powder. Fortunately, we found the Berley Lakes just before night fell. With the renewed good cheer that accompanies victory, we tramped out a flat spot, set up the tent, and snuggled into our sleeping bags for a long winter's nap.

During that night however, while we slumbered as if dead, it snowed two and a half feet. A thick white comforter of snow settled over the tent.

The next morning we nearly failed to wake up. I recall gasping groggily in the dark, my brain swirling. All I wanted to do was close my eyes and drift into oblivion. Was this the confusion of the Berley Lakes vortex?

I still can't remember which one of us managed to rise from his sleeping bag and summon the strength to start digging out.

The snow had buried our tent so thoroughly that we had no air. Lack of oxygen had left us disoriented.

When we finally clawed our way out of the dark snow dome and stood blinking at the sunshine, we marveled at how close we had come to asphyxiation.

I couldn't help but wonder what would have happened if we had not woken up. In all probability, searchers would not have

Getting There: Drive Highway 20 to Santiam Pass. If you're skiing, park at the Santiam Sno Play area at the northwest side of the summit. A Sno-Park permit is required here, available at outdoor stores. If you're hiking, park at the Pacific Crest Trailhead at the northeast side of the summit. A Northwest Forest Pass is required to park here. It can be purchased at outdoor stores and ranger stations.

Season: Ski season runs December through April. Hiking season is July through October.

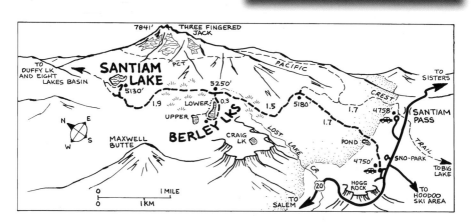

found us in this remote location until the snow had melted off the tent.

Imagine how puzzled the searchers would have been, discovering three dead men, with no signs of trauma, peacefully laid out in warm sleeping bags in a cozy, hurricane-proof tent.

The mystery would only have added to the Berley Lakes' reputation.

The outlet of Lower Berley Lake.

After this frightening introduction, you may be wondering why I am now going to describe how you, too, can ski or hike into this Bermuda Triangle.

The answer is that a new generation of GPS devices has made destinations like the Berley Lakes more achievable. The route is still confusing. You will still need to take the basic survival gear that you should always pack when venturing into the wilderness. Route-finding and map-reading skills will always be important. But with satellites tracking your progress on a hand-held GPS device, your chances of finding the lake are much better.

Until recently, GPS devices did not work in forested areas where trees can block the view of satellites. This made the handheld locators useless on most western Oregon trails.

Today you can buy a GPS device with a high-power antenna that works even when you're indoors in a basement. For an additional charge you can load the device's memory chip with hundreds of detailed topographic

The Berley Lakes fill a small hidden glen that has no marked trails, and is easy to miss.

Three Fingered Jack from Lower Berley Lake in winter.

maps covering the entire state.

In summer the need for this kind of high-powered navigation equipment is lower because the danger of freezing to death is lower.

With an ordinary map and compass in hand, experienced hikers can simply drive to the Pacific Crest Trailhead at Santiam Pass, follow the PCT 3.2 miles north to a crest with a small campsite, and take a small trail to the left along a dry, rocky creekbed 200 yards to Lower Berley Lake.

In winter the PCT trailhead is snowed under, so you'll need to start at the Santiam Pass Snow Play area instead. It's on the north side of the highway, just east of the turnoff for the Hoodoo ski area.

Start at the right-hand edge of the parking loop, put on your skis or snowshoes, and tromp 50 feet to the base of the snow play hill. Traverse to the left, angling slightly uphill into the burned woods. Then head due north.

You may see tree blazes along the way because this is the old Skyline Trail, a route that predated the Pacific Crest Trail. After the 2003 fire, the Forest Service abandoned this convenient stretch of trail because so many burned trees had fallen across the path. In winter, the old trail still works fine.

OREGON FAVORITES

Don't expect signs or markers. Because this is wilderness, the blue plastic diamonds used to mark snow trails elsewhere are not allowed.

After 1.7 miles you'll join the PCT, although the signpost here will probably be buried under snow. Next you'll want to contour to the left (the west) for half a mile to avoid climbing a ridge. When you get around the ridge, turn north again for a mile.

On this stretch you'll cross a small, snow-covered meadow. This was the site of Jack Shelter, an open-sided building used by early rangers in the days when forest patrols were often on horseback. Like Sunshine Shelter at the foot of North Sister, this shelter burned shortly after passage of the 1964 Wilderness Act.

If you keep heading north you'll eventually climb to a small forested pass (GPS location N 44° 27.576' W 121° 52.370'). Here you'll need to turn left along a snow-covered creekbed, plowing your way through a snowy thicket 200 yards to Lower Berley Lake (GPS location N 44° 27.539' W 121° 52.464').

When it's iced over in winter, this long, narrow lake resembles a white golf fairway with a dogleg to the right. At the far end, the view of Three Fingered Jack's snowy crags is so spectacular that I used it on the cover of my *Atlas of Oregon Wilderness*.

The second of the two lakes, Upper Berley Lake, is somewhere nearby, but I've only found it once. I don't have a GPS reading for the upper lake, and to be honest, I don't want one.

Every wilderness needs a little mystery.

Three Fingered Jack from Lower Berley Lake in summer.

April
In Oregon

ONEONTA GORGE

Wood violet. At left: Oneonta Gorge.

For years Oregon's number one tourist goal was our tallest cascade, Multnomah Falls. What am I supposed to think now that our most visited attraction is the Spirit Mountain Casino?

Actually, I think Multnomah Falls is still too crowded.

If you're going to gamble on an April outing I'd place my bets on Oneonta Creek, the gorge next door. The path here explores a cavern behind a waterfall, and then loops around a mossy chasm so narrow that Oneonta Creek fills it wall to wall. A short detour upstream takes you to Triple Falls, where three plumes of water plunge 120 feet at once.

That's a three-of-a-kind deal to beat anything in the casino.

Even the parking lot for the Oneonta Creek loop has a great view. The trail sets out beside 176-foot Horsetail Falls, climbing along a mossy slope of little licorice ferns. Tiny white candyflowers and pink geraniums crowd the path in April.

After a quarter mile turn right on the Gorge Trail, which soon ducks behind 80-foot Ponytail Falls (alias Upper Horsetail Falls). The lava flow that created this falls' stony lip also buried a layer of soft soil. The falls have washed out the underlying soil, creating the cavern.

Half a mile beyond the falls, take a right-hand fork for a quick viewpoint loop out to a cliff edge high above the highway. The view extends up the Columbia to Beacon Rock, but keep children away from the unfenced edge.

Then continue on the main trail another half mile, switchback down to a dramatic metal

Getting There: Drive Interstate 84 east of Portland to Ainsworth Park exit 35 and follow the old scenic highway 1.5 miles back to the large Horsetail Falls Trailhead parking area.

Triple Falls.

footbridge above 60-foot Oneonta Falls, and climb to a junction with the Oneonta Trail.

Turn left here if you'd like to take the optional side trip up to Triple Falls. It's a perfect spot for lunch, at a footbridge in a scenic creekside glen at the top of the falls. If you're hiking with children, however, you'd best skip Triple Falls and simply turn right to continue the loop. Follow the Oneonta Trail a mile down to the highway and walk along the road to the mouth of slot-like Oneonta Gorge.

With any luck you'll be able to lounge here on the creek's pebble beach while one of your party runs up the road another third of a mile to fetch the car. While you're lounging, notice the old tunnel entrance in the gorge's wall, the original route of the old Columbia River Highway.

You might also be tempted to venture up the gorge's slot. The chasm ends half a mile upstream at the base of 100-foot Oneonta Falls, but you have to wade a lot along the way. This is a reasonable challenge for adventurers in September when the creek is warm and shallow. In April, when the water is waist deep and icy, it's enough to admire the gorge while lounging beside the highway bridge.

Springtime at Oneonta Gorge is flush with wildflowers, waterfalls, and green. And that's a bet you can take to the bank.

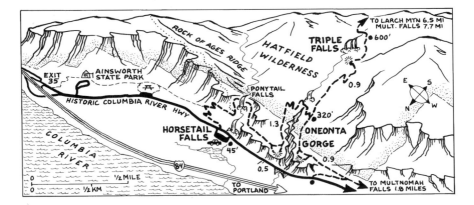

OREGON FAVORITES

ASTORIA'S TWO CENTURIES

The Astor Column.

Spruced up for its 200th anniversary, Astoria deserves more than a drive-by camera shooting. Spend the weekend and plan a stroll to see the waterfront promenade, the gingerbread mansions of old town, and the shops of the revitalized commercial district.

The oldest permanent United States settlement this side of the Mississippi, Astoria clings like a barnacle to the Oregon shore of the Columbia River. Wars, boomtimes, and countless winter storms have overswept this tenacious town since 1811, when fur traders built a stockade here.

Today Astoria is Oregon's only port of call for cruise ships. Each week in summer the floating white hotels flood downtown with thousands of tourists in search of souvenirs, espresso drinks, microbrews, and history.

If you're arriving by land, start your tour at the Columbia River

Tickets to the Columbia Maritime Museum include boarding passes to a lighthouse ship.

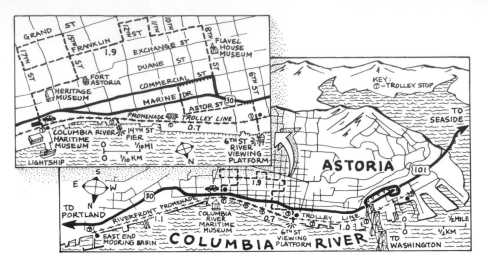

Maritime Museum, on the waterfront at 17th Street.

Inside this first-rate interpretive center you can spin the wheel of a replica steamboat pilothouse, walk the bridge of a World War II destroyer, or watch the rotating prisms of a lighthouse's lens. Other exhibits feature shipwrecks, fishing, and early exploration.

Museum admission includes a boarding pass to the adjacent lightship *Columbia.* This unusual ship served as a floating lighthouse at the river's entrance until 1979.

In front of the museum you'll pass a trolley stop for "Old 300," a restored 1913 San Antonio streetcar that runs the length of the waterfront. A promenade follows the trolley route, so you can either walk or ride the next eleven blocks, heading west past docks, shops, offices, restaurants, and fish-packing plants. At Sixth Street detour briefly to the right to climb a viewing platform on a pier beside the river's main shipping channel.

Then head inland through Astoria's business district. Highlights here

The Flavel House, built by a wealthy Columbia River bar pilot, is now a museum.

Astoria's waterfront promenade over-looks the Astoria-Megler bridge.

include passing some of Astoria's prettiest "painted ladies" — colorful Victorian homes. The route also passes a replica stockade tower built on the site of the original Fort Astoria (15th and Exchange), where the city began in 1811.

Most of the original fort's site is now occupied by the Fort George Brewery & Public House, which, along with the Wet Dog Cafe & Astoria Brewing Company near the promenade on 11th, offer microbrews for hikers heading home.

Astoria has held out here for two centuries. Visitors should give this heroic outpost at least two days.

Getting There: The Columbia River Maritime Museum is at Highway 30 and 17th Street on Astoria's waterfront (1.5 miles east of the Columbia River bridge). Hours are 9:30am to 5pm daily.

Tips for Visitors: The waterfront trolley costs about $1 and passes the museum about every 45 minutes in summer (weekdays 3pm-9pm, weekends noon-9pm). The rest of the year it runs Friday to Sunday noon-6pm.

The Flavel House Museum at 441 8th Street is open daily from 10am to 5pm (winter 11am-4pm). Clementine's Bed & Breakfast, at 847 Exchange, takes reservations at *www.clementines-bb.com* or 800-521-6801.

The best viewpoint of Astoria is atop the 125-foot Astor Tower. To find it, turn off Highway 30 at 16th Street and follow signs.

9

GOOD NEWS FOR BADLANDS

Many of Oregon's wilderness getaways are under snow in April, but not the Badlands. In fact, this strange lava landscape southeast of Bend is at its best in spring, when the desert blooms.

Hiking the Badlands is an otherworldly experience. There are no creeks, lakes, or mountains. Instead the area is a labyrinth of lava outcrops and sandy openings, crossed by an eerie, dead river that has been dry since the Ice Age.

The fresh-looking lava here erupted from the flanks of the Newberry Volcano 10,000 years ago. The liquid rock puddled up in a prairie and then buckled into thousands of ten-foot-tall pressure ridges—in much the same way that a sloppy paint job will wrinkle as it dries.

Later the cataclysmic eruption of Mt. Mazama (which created Crater Lake) blanketed this area with a foot of volcanic ash, filling in the low spots. The result is a maze of what appear to be sandy trails bordered by lava walls.

It may be the most confusing place I have ever hiked. Every sandy trail looks real, but most are meandering madness. I needed a GPS device just to get back to my car.

The secret of success is to follow ancient Jeep tracks. Now that motorized vehicles are banned, the parallel ruts of old roads provide the area's only reliable trails.

Bring lots of water and pack a compass or GPS device. It's also wise to wear layers of clothing. In springtime the high desert can quickly shift from chilly to hot. If you wait to visit until summer, beware of sunstroke. Then you'll need to avoid the midday heat and wear a big sun hat.

One of the best hikes follows a nearly level trail to Flatiron Rock, a fortress-shaped outcrop with natural rock windows. Sagebrush and gnarled juniper trees dominate the route. The trees are hardly 20 feet tall, but can be

At left, faint red petroglyphs remain in a cave along the Dry River's channel. Above: Oregon sunshine blooms in spring.

thousands of years old. The oldest tree in Oregon is very likely here.

When you reach the 30-foot outcrop of Flatiron Rock, turn left on a steep sandy path that climbs to the rock castle's parapet, where 10-foot walls line a maze of paths. Keep right around the summit of Flatiron Rock to a viewpoint of distant Mt. Jefferson. Then continue counter-clockwise around the summit to find a natural arch in a 20-foot pillar. Just beyond, where two slots join, keep left to complete a loop around Flatiron Rock's top.

Monkeyflower.

Another excellent hike in the Badlands Wilderness visits a channel of the vanished Dry River. During the Ice Age a tributary of the Deschutes River drained a vast lake on the present site of Millican. The stream cut through Dry River Canyon and snaked across this lava landscape.

The hike to the Dry River channel sets out from the Badlands Rock Trailhead on an old dirt road that's closed to motor vehicles. Walk 0.3 mile to a fork in the road. You'll want to go right here, but first explore the sagebrush area to the left to see a homestead from the early 1900s. A wire fence protects an old cistern. All artifacts are federally protected.

Then take the right-hand fork at the homestead and continue 0.9 mile. Leave the road when you reach three large boulders on the right. Take

Getting There: For Flatiron Rock, drive 16 miles east of Bend on Highway 20 toward Burns. At milepost 16 turn left across a yellow cattle guard to the Flatiron Trailhead, a rough dirt parking turnaround (GPS location N43 57.454' W121 03.086').

Hiking Tips for Flatiron Rock: From the right-hand edge of the parking area, walk past some boulders 30 feet to a fork in the trail. To the left is the return route of an optional loop. Turn right on an ancient sandy roadbed that veers near the highway before heading north. After 1.3 miles, veer left at the start of a large triangle where trails meet. At the next junction, a hundred steps farther, go straight. Beyond the triangle 1.6 miles you'll reach the 30-foot outcrop of Flatiron Rock (GPS location N43 59.362' W121 02.748').

For the Dry River Channel: Drive Highway 20 east of the Flatiron Trailhead 1.5 miles (or east of Bend 18 miles). At the bottom of a hill, turn left on an unmarked paved road for one mile. Then turn left into the dirt Badlands Rock Trailhead (GPS location N43 57.216' W121 00.883'). Walk 0.3 mile, fork right, and continue 0.9 mile until you see three large boulders on the right (GPS location N43 57.788' W121 00.286'). Leave the road here and go 100 yards down to the right to a pole fence at the entrance to the Dry River's channel.

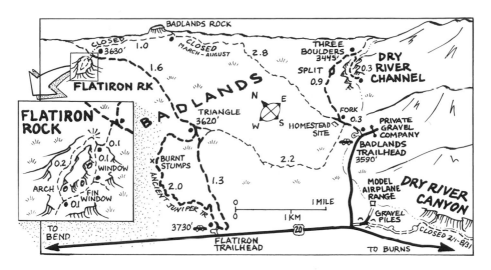

Map labels:
BADLANDS ROCK
CLOSED ● 3630' 1.0
CLOSED MARCH–AUGUST 2.8
THREE BOULDERS 3445'
DRY RIVER CHANNEL
1.6
SPLIT 0.3
0.9
FLATIRON RK
B A D L A N D S
TRIANGLE 3620'
N E W S
FORK 0.3
HOMESTEAD SITE
PRIVATE GRAVEL COMPANY
BADLANDS TRAILHEAD 3590'
FLATIRON ROCK
0.1
0.1 WINDOW
ARCH 0.2 0.1 FIN WINDOW 0.1
BURNT STUMPS
ANCIENT JUNIPER TR 2.0
1.3
2.2
MODEL AIRPLANE RANGE
DRY RIVER CANYON
GRAVEL PILES
TO BEND
3730'
0 1 MILE
0 1 KM
20
FLATIRON TRAILHEAD
TO BURNS
CLOSED 2/1–8/31

a track down to the right to a pole fence at the mouth of the Dry River's channel. Beyond is a narrow canyon with 40-foot rock walls.

An overhang to the right served as a cave campsite when the river ran with fish, perhaps 6000 years ago. The faint red ochre petroglyphs here can be damaged even by the oil of fingerprints, so don't touch!

No one today can interpret these petroglyphs precisely, but similar symbols were often left at sites where people hunted or fished. One explanation is that the petroglyphs were an appeal to the animals' spirits, encouraging them to return. If so, the appeal backfired here. Not only did the fish vanish, but the river did too.

Most artifacts in Oregon museums tell of our history since statehood in 1859. Here in the Badlands you see the truth, that our history is measured not in centuries, but millennia.

The summit of Flatiron Rock resembles a castle with rock palisades and natural windows.

10
TABLE ROCKS' FORTRESS

Joseph Lane, the U.S. senator who gave Lane County its name, won his reputation for bravery with a daring hike into an Indian stronghold atop Lower Table Rock.

Today this dramatic mesa near Medford still looks daunting, but the modern trail to the top is easy enough that hikers with children can usually manage it. On weekends in April and May, the agencies that own the rock usually even offer free guided tours.

Thanks to the intense efforts of public-spirited conservationists, Lower Table Rock has become a haven for hikers—and for the endangered

A Takelma stronghold in the Rogue River Indian War, Lower Table Rock remains sacred to the tribe.   Above: Clarkia amoena *is known as Farewell to Spring.*

wildflower species that bloom here in profusion each spring.

When real estate speculators proposed a subdivision inside Lower Table Rock's bowl in 1979, The Nature Conservancy raised $500,000 to save it. The Bureau of Land Management has since formed a partnership with this public-spirited non-profit group, building trails and designating additional land. In 2009 The Nature Conservancy bought the last private land on the two mesas for $3.9 million.

Today each mesa has its own trail. From a trailside viewpoint on Lower Table Rock's lofty rim, the Rogue River seems to writhe like a great green snake across suburban Medford's orchards, ranches, and gravel pit ponds. The distant white cone of Mt. McLoughlin gleams from the horizon. Turkey vultures soar on updrafts from the plateau's cliffs.

In Oregon's pioneer days, the local Takelma tribe retreated here to use the mesa as a natural fortress against the area's increasingly hostile white settlers. To this day, the mesas remain sacred to the Takelmas.

In the tribe's language, *takelma* means "those who live along the river." The river they traditionally lived along was the Rogue, in the valley between present-day Ashland and Grants Pass. The Gold Rush of 1849 sent thousands of white miners trekking south from the Willamette Valley to California. The Takelmas responded to this flood of unruly travelers by demanding payment in goods for passage across their land.

In the summer of 1851, the U.S. Army sent a survey patrol to "clear the road" of hostile Indians between Oregon and California. The Takelmas spotted the troops first and shot one soldier from his saddle. The Army called for reinforcements. The new troops didn't attack the warriors. Instead they simply took thirty Takelma women and children hostage. The Takelmas quickly agreed to peace, and the hostages were released.

That tenuous peace agreement took a blow five months later, when two packers discovered gold in a creek at Jacksonville. Suddenly thousands of miners swarmed into Southern Oregon, churning up the salmon streams and shooting deer for food. With game scarce, the hungry Takelmas suffered miserably during the cold winter of 1852-53. When two Takelma men tried to exchange gold for food in a town they were summarily shot, on the assumption that their gold must have been stolen from white miners.

The winds of war picked up speed the next summer. On August 3, 1853, a settler was found dead from hatchet wounds in a cabin on Bear Creek, south of present-day Medford. Two days later a packer was ambushed at dusk and fatally wounded on the outskirts of Jacksonville.

Jacksonville townspeople didn't know who was responsible for the attacks. But by August 6, an angry mob of miners called for revenge against all the area's Indians. The mob hanged two Shasta tribesmen who happened to be in town from California. A few days later, a group of volunteers arrived from Crescent City under a homemade banner that read, "Extermination!"

Buoyed by the Crescent City recruits, the mob in Jacksonville formed a ragtag militia of twenty-two men and sallied forth to wage war. The Takelmas, however, were ready. They ambushed the volunteers on August 17, killing two men and capturing eighteen horses loaded with guns and ammunition. That same day, Takelmas attacked settlers and travelers throughout the Rogue Valley, killing six.

The U.S. Army agreed to join forces with the volunteers on August 21. Under the command of Joe Lane they fought a bloody but indecisive battle with the Takelmas in the hills north of the Table Rocks. Lane himself took a rifle ball through his shoulder. Before the Army could regroup for another attack, seven hundred Takelmas slipped away and climbed a narrow trail up past the cliffs ringing Lower Table Rock.

To the soldiers left on the plains below, this horseshoe-shaped mesa must have looked as unassailable as an island in the sky. The tribes' rifles bristled from the rimrock. Days passed as the Army men debated how to dislodge the Takelmas from Lower Table Rock. A frontal attack on the cliffs was obviously hopeless, and a siege might take months.

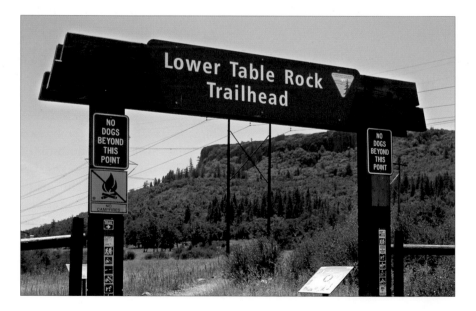

Lower Table Rock overlooks the Rogue River and the Siskiyou Mountains.

Finally Joe Lane decided he would try diplomacy. On September 10 he rebandaged his wounded shoulder, recruited an intrepid interpreter, left his weapons behind, and walked up toward Lower Table Rock under a flag of truce. Few men thought he would come back alive.

Today as you hike the trail, the wildflowers along the way make it easy to forget, for a time at least, the tension of Joe Lane's daring 1853 walk.

In spring the scrub oak grassland here is ablaze with blooms. In April you'll see blue camas and pink fawn lilies. In May look for pink, four-petaled clarkias (alias "farewell to spring"), California blue-eyed grass (with six small petals), and elegant brodiaea (with six long purple petals). By June, orange paintbrush and purple crown brodiaea are blooming too.

While you're climbing, you'll have a nice view across the plain to Upper Table Rock, an almost identical U-shaped mesa a few miles east. The 125-foot-thick andesite rims capping these mesas are remnants of a lava flow that poured down the Rogue River Valley 7 million years ago from a vent near Lost Creek Lake. Since then, erosion has worn away the softer surrounding rock, leaving the hard andesite perched 800 feet above the plain.

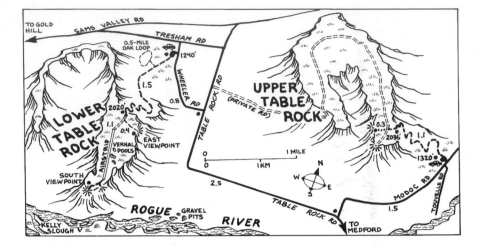

A good place to return to Joe Lane's 1853 drama is where the path suddenly crests at the plateau. When Lane reached this summit he was surrounded by seven hundred wary Takelmas. The warriors wore stripes of white war paint on their foreheads, a decoration betokening the grizzly bear. Men and women alike wore bones, shells, and leather straps through their pierced noses and ears. The tribe took Lane under heavy guard to a parley site overlooking the valley to the south.

As you hike across the plateau to this viewpoint today you'll walk the length of an abandoned, grassy airstrip. Look alongside the old runway for "vernal pools" — ponds that dry up by May, leaving a haze of flowers. Some of the blooms are dwarf meadowfoam, a rare subspecies that exists only on the Table Rocks. At the airstrip's end, continue right on a path to the cliff-edged parley point, towering above the Rogue River.

Here Joe Lane looked down to see his Army dragoons drawn up on the plain below, hopelessly out of reach. Through his interpreter he began negotiating with the Takelma leaders. He seemed to be making progress toward a settlement when a naked warrior dashed into the encampment with news that miners on the Applegate River had tied a Dakubetede man to a tree and killed him. Suddenly the Takelmas grabbed their weapons and began clamoring to tie Joe Lane to a tree and kill him in revenge.

Through his interpreter, Lane gave a speech that saved his life. He promised to find the guilty miners and punish them. He pointed to the Army troops below and said if the Takelmas killed him, more soldiers would come to attack the tribe. He offered to set aside Lower Table Rock and the lands to the north as a reservation. He promised to build an Army fort nearby to protect the tribe from white vigilantes.

The Takelma leaders calmed their warriors, listened to the sobering words of this courageous white man, and before the day was out, agreed to peace on Lane's terms.

Joe Lane became a hero among both the Oregon tribes and the white settlers. The Table Rock Reservation was ratified as promised. The Army built Fort Lane across the river from Lower Table Rock as agreed, reassuring both the tribe and the settlers for the time being.

Ookow.

Catapulted by his fame, Lane won election to the U.S. Senate and became the namesake for a newly designated Oregon county. In 1860, Lane was nominated for Vice President of the United States. The famous diplomat of Lower Table Rock might well have won that prize—and might even have become President one day—if he had not been running against the ticket of an Illinois lawyer named Lincoln.

As for the Takelmas, they were attacked again by a ragtag band of white miners in 1855. This time the miners sneaked onto the Table Rock Reservation and fired into a sleeping village below Table Rock. After nearly a year of skirmishes, the surviving Takelma tribespeople were shipped to reservations on the northern Oregon Coast and Coast Range.

Stories of Oregon's Indian wars never end happily. But as you stand on the edge of Lower Table Rock's rim, it's comforting to remember that day long ago when the Takelmas held their ground and the heroes were the peacemakers.

Getting There: To find Lower Table Rock from Interstate 5 just north of Medford, take Central Point exit 33, drive east on Biddle Road 1 mile, turn left on Table Rock Road 7.7 miles to the "10" milepost marker, and turn left on Wheeler Road 0.8 mile to a parking area on the left. To find the Upper Table Rock trailhead instead, drive back toward Medford 2.5 miles on Table Rock Road and turn left on Modoc Road for 1.5 miles to a parking lot on the left.

Hiking Tips: Hiking distance is 5.2 miles round trip to Lower Table Rock's viewpoint, with 780 feet of elevation gain, and 2.8 miles round-trip to Upper Table Rock's summit, gaining 720 feet of elevation. Dogs, horses, fires, and flower picking are banned in this nature preserve. Also beware of poison oak alongside the trail. For information about the free, guided hikes led here on April and May weekends, call the Medford BLM office at 541-618-2200.

MAY
IN OREGON

CAPE HORN PRESERVED

Columbia River tides still lap against the basalt cliffs of Cape Horn, precisely as they did more than 200 years ago, when Lewis & Clark paddled past in the spring of 1806.

To see this riverside landmark for yourself, try the spectacular trail that loops around the bluff on the Washington side of the Columbia Gorge, 26 miles east of Vancouver.

A short version of the hike is lovely in April, when wildflowers run riot on viewpoint bluffs. To protect nesting falcons, the full loop is open only from July through December.

Cape Horn remains untouched by the dams and freeways that have changed much of the Columbia Gorge. Even the railroad on the Washington side of the river is hidden in a tunnel behind this cliff.

The most serious threat to Cape Horn's natural look came in the 1990s, when private developers offered twelve large homesites for sale atop the bluff. Outraged activists, determined to save the Columbia Gorge from overdevelopment, started buying the lots for the public. Only one mansion was actually built here — and it too was later bought and removed.

Surprisingly, one of the leaders in the battle to save Cape Horn was a real estate developer. Dan Huntington of Washougal convinced the non-profit Columbia Land Trust to raise millions of dollars to buy land and easements — despite opposition from Skamania County commissioners who favored private ownership.

Next Huntington asked the U. S. Forest Service to help build a trail. Although the USFS controls most of the rest of Cape Horn, they refused.

Unfazed, Huntington rallied volunteers to do the job themselves. It took them seven years to rough out a 7-mile loop trail across the bluff. The path climbed to clifftop viewpoints, overlooked a train tunnel entrance, and even ducked behind a waterfall.

At left, the trail up Cape Horn is crowded in May by blue larkspur and pink bleeding hearts. Above, the view from Pioneer Point.

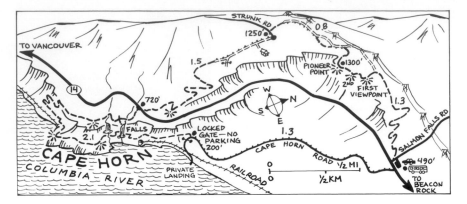

It was one of the most beautiful hikes in the Columbia Gorge.

The route became so popular that the Forest Service finally stepped in. Their planners redesigned the homemade path, widening the tread, improving the grade, and replacing highway crossings with pedestrian tunnels. They also closed the lower half of the loop from January through June to protect nesting birds.

To visit, start by driving (or taking a Skamania County bus) to a Park & Ride lot beside Cape Horn on Highway 14. Then walk across Salmon Creek Road. The path climbs amid a lush bigleaf maple forest with sword ferns and vine maple. April brings a profusion of flowers: four-foot-tall stalks of blue larkspur, red bleeding hearts, and pink-striped candyflower.

After crossing a small creek the path switchbacks up a mile to the first of three cliff-edge viewpoints overlooking the Columbia Gorge. Note Wahkeena Falls on the far shore, a mile upriver. The broad, wooded arc of Larch Mountain is on the horizon. The little crag in the river below you is Phoca Rock.

At the third and highest viewpoint, Pioneer Point, blue camas flowers

Tidewater laps at cliffs below the Cape Horn trail.

The lower portion of the trail (closed January through June) passes a train tunnel.

seem to sprout straight out of the rock. This makes a good turnaround point for a short spring hike.

If it's after July 1 and you're game for the full 7-mile loop, continue onward. The trail crosses a broad, wooded summit and joins an abandoned road. This is part of a historic wagon route from Vancouver through the Columbia Gorge. After another 0.6 mile you'll reach paved Strunk Road. Walk left on this street 200 feet to its end and turn right on the first gravel driveway. This lane turns grassy and eventually becomes a trail down through the woods to a crossing of Highway 14.

The trail below the highway crosses two creeks in the woods before switchbacking down a rockslide to the top of a railroad tunnel. Freight trains vanish beneath you into Cape Horn.

The next mile of the trail is a hiker's amusement ride, roller-coasting up and down along the riverside cliffs, ducking behind a waterfall, and popping out at unexpected viewpoints. The fun ends at Cape Horn Road.

Getting There: Drive Interstate 5 north across the Columbia River bridge and turn right on Highway 14 for 26 miles through Camas and Washougal. Between mileposts 26 and 27, turn left on Salmon Falls Road and immediately turn right into the Park & Ride lot on the right. Then walk across Salmon Falls Road to find the trail.

Because there's no room to park a shuttle car here, you have to walk 1.3 miles up the paved road to complete the loop.

Considering how close Cape Horn lies to the Portland-Vancouver megalopolis, a surprising amount of the scenery remains as it was during Lewis and Clark's exploration. Saving this scenery for the public was a worthy battle indeed.

12

CLARK AT TILLAMOOK HEAD

My favorite Lewis and Clark hike is the scenic trail across Tillamook Head where the Corps of Discovery went looking for a whale.

This 8-mile-long, cliff-edge path above the ocean looks much as it did 200 years ago, when it inspired Clark to exclaim in wonder. His praise makes perfect sense, even today, but his decision to look for a whale in this vicinity needs some explanation.

After Lewis and Clark's first sighting of the Pacific Ocean at the mouth of the Columbia River in November, 1805, they decided to spend the winter a few miles inland, where it was less stormy. They chose a clearing on what became known as the Lewis and Clark River, a lazy backwater six miles south of present-day Astoria.

Soon the whole group was busily building a fifty-foot-square log stockade. They finished in a mere two weeks. They dubbed the camp Fort Clatsop in honor of the tribe that ruled the lower Columbia.

Rain fell on all but twelve of the 106 dreary days the expedition spent at Fort Clatsop. They celebrated Christmas listlessly with what Clark described as "pore Elk, so much Spoiled that we eate it thro' mear necessity. Some Spoiled pounded fish and a fiew roots."

By January Clark was arguing with Lewis over the need for salt to preserve and spice their meager fare. Perhaps sensing his cabin fever, Lewis let Clark lead an excursion to Killamuck, a beachside village of friendly Clatsops. There, a hundred feet from what is now the

Haystack Rock at Cannon Beach. At left below, Indian Beach in Ecola State Park.

Promenade in the city of Seaside, he boiled seawater in five large kettles, obtaining nearly a gallon of salt a day. The site is now a Seaside city park, with a replica of Clark's kiln.

While unwinding at this beach retreat, Clark heard from locals that a whale was stranded at the next village south, on the other side of Tillamook Head. He passed word back to Lewis at Fort Clatsop that tribespeople from up and down the coast were going to help butcher the whale—should he go too? Oil was also lacking in the expedition's diet, and the beached whale's blubber might provide a source.

As soon as Sacajawea heard the news, she begged to go along. "She observed that she had traveled a long way with us to see the great waters," Lewis wrote, "and now that monstrous fish was also to be seen, she thought it very hard she could not be permitted to see either."

So Sacajawea joined Clark and a small group of men on a mossy rainforest trail tracing the edge of Tillamook Head's colossal cliff—essentially the same path that crosses Ecola State Park from Seaside today.

Clark gazed back across a twenty-mile sweep of wilderness beach to the distant blue of Cape Disappointment, and later wrote, "I beheld the grandest and most pleasing prospects which my eyes ever surveyed."

A modern trailside sign commemorates a likely location for "Clark's Point of View."

On the far side of Tillamook Head, Clark's group followed the beach

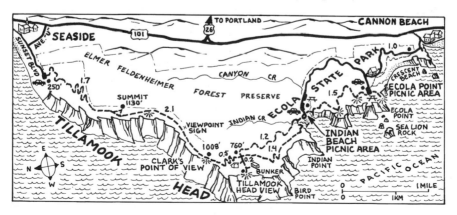

The lighthouse on Tillamook Rock, a mile offshore, was once used by a mortuary.

two miles to a cluster of five huts, the forerunner of Cannon Beach's crowded mishmash of artsy boutiques and motels.

There, beside a creek, lay the skeleton of a 105-foot whale. Unfortunately for Clark, the entire animal had already been dissected for meat or blubber, and the locals weren't keen on sharing. Clark had to bargain hard to get a mere three hundred pounds of blubber and a few gallons of whale oil, which the group then lugged back to Fort Clatsop.

When you hike across Tillamook Head today, you'll see two features Clark could not. One is an abandoned six-room concrete bunker that housed a radar installation in World War II. The other is Oregon's strangest lighthouse, a desolate tower a mile offshore on a small, barren island

A concrete bunker remains from a World War II radar station on the headland's tip.

named Tillamook Rock.

Dubbed "Terrible Tilly" by the crews who staffed it, this wave-swept lighthouse outpost was built in 1881, abandoned in 1934, and sold as surplus government property in 1957. More recently it belonged to Eternity At Sea, a now-defunct funeral business that catered to people who want to be stored in a lighthouse when they die.

Free backpacker shelters on Tillamook Head.

A moderate 3-mile loop samples Tillamook Head's sights. The trail from the Indian Beach picnic area follows an old roadbed through a rainforest of alders and ancient spruces. Near the headland's crest you'll reach a backpackers' camping area that features three open-sided log shelters. Although these Adirondack-style huts aren't what Lewis and Clark used, they give you the general idea.

You'll find a four-way trail crossing by the shelters. To see the concrete bunker and viewpoint of Tillamook Rock, go straight. If you'd rather just return to your car on a loop, go left.

And if you'd like to spend a night like Lewis and Clark, grab a bunk in the shelters. There is no charge to stay here, as long as you've paid the day use fee for your car at the trailhead. Just as in 1806, campers don't have to book in advance.

Getting There: Drive Highway 101 south of Seaside 7 miles to the first Cannon Beach exit. Follow signs to Ecola State Park, keeping right for 2 miles to the park's entrance booth. Expect a $5-per-car day use fee here. Throughout the park, dogs must be on leash.

Hiking Tips: For a quick sample of the park's scenery, turn left at the entrance booth, park at the far left-hand end of the Ecola Point picnic area, and walk 200 yards out a paved path to a viewpoint deck.

For longer hikes at Tillamook Head it's best to start at the Indian Beach picnic area. Drive there by turning right at the park's fee booth for 1.5 miles. The trail starts behind the restroom on the right. After 200 feet ignore a footbridge to the left. Keep straight on the main trail 1.2 miles to a trail crossing by three camping shelters. Continue straight 0.2 mile to the concrete bunker and viewpoint at the headland's tip. To return on a loop, walk back to the camp shelters and turn right.

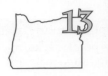

13

ZUMWALT PRAIRIE

Two little-known treasures on the edge of Hells Canyon tempt travelers to visit the extreme northeast corner of Oregon before summer — Buckhorn Lookout and Zumwalt Prairie.

Hawks and eagles circle above Zumwalt Prairie, between the snowy Wallowa Mountains and the ragged cliffs of Hells Canyon. This rolling grassland has one of the highest concentrations of breeding raptors in the world, largely because the native bunchgrass prairie here teems with their favorite prey, ground squirrels.

Oregon State University researcher Marcy Houle celebrated the area's rich ecosystem in her 1995 book, *The Prairie Keepers*. She marveled that a century of careful cattle grazing may actually have improved raptor habitat.

This intrigued The Nature Conservancy, a nonprofit group that likes to preserve land and build partnerships with locals. The group bought 51 square miles here. It's now the largest private nature preserve in the state.

Most of the preserve is off limits, but the Nature Conservancy has opened a couple of short, easy hiking routes that show off the prairie's birds, flowers, and views.

If you're driving all the way to Zumwalt Prairie, however, you really shouldn't miss the nearby Buckhorn fire lookout. Perched right on the lip of Hells Canyon, this historic cabin may well have the best panorama of the colossal chasm—especially since a fire overswept the more famous Hat Point lookout in 2007. That fire destroyed viewpoint decks, picnic tables, and most trees at Hat Point. The 90-foot lookout tower at Hat Point survived only because firefighters wrapped it with fireproof Kevlar paper before the flames arrived.

As you drive across Zumwalt Prairie you'll see the weathered barns of homesteaders who tried to settle this arid upland. Among those settlers were Henry and Josie Zumwalt, who opened a post office here in 1903.

The road across the prairie climbs 30 miles to Buckhorn Lookout. Snow can block the upper portion of the route until late May.

At the lookout itself, the vast canyons of the Imnaha River steal the show. The Snake River is hidden, but look for Idaho's snow-capped Seven Devils above Hat Point's plateau, and the long white horizon of the Wallowa Mountains above Zumwalt Prairie.

With a view like this, the 14-foot-square lookout building never needed a tower, so it sits on the ground. Built in the 1930s, the building is no longer staffed.

Although a trail near Buckhorn Lookout does descend to the Snake River, that path is faint and loses a staggering 4000 feet of elevation. For an easier hike, drive back to Zumwalt Prairie. The two trails there are so easy you can do them both in the same afternoon.

The Wildrye Trail ambles across the nature preserve to a pond. The second hiking route at Zumwalt Prairie scrambles up Harsin Butte for a look around. These trails are prettiest from late March to early June when wildflowers bloom and the hawks are hunting. There's not much point to come here in August. That may be the busiest season for trails in the nearby Wallowa Mountains, but summer leaves the prairie brown and dead.

The Buckhorn Lookout (above) has a view across Imnaha River canyonlands (below).

Start the Wildrye Trail at a brown metal gate with a small orange sign. The trail is a faint old roadbed straight ahead, striking off across the prairie.

The big horizon is empty, save for the humps of Harsin and Findley Buttes. The real view is at your feet, where you'll see six kinds of native grasses, including 5-foot clumps of basin wildrye. Look for the blooms of yellow bells in April, pink Nootka roses and yellow lupine in May, and pink Clarkia and white mariposa lilies in June.

The Nature Conservancy burns this area periodically to boost native plants, including the threatened Spaldings catchfly, an unobtrusive white-petaled flower that can catch flies with its sticky leaves.

After a mile or so the Wildrye Trail peters out at the (possibly dry) swale of Camp Creek, which you can follow left to a teardrop-shaped pond with dragonflies, cattails, and wild mint. Then return as you came.

For the second hike, you drive a few miles of rough ranch roads to a cattle guard near the base of Harsin Butte. Then park beside the road, walk across the cattle guard, and head toward Harsin Butte. Although there is no trail up this rounded knoll, it's the only high ground for miles, so there's not much chance of confusion.

A pond along the Wildrye Trail.

The route steepens as it passes a ponderosa pine grove where elk like to bed. The wildflowers bloom later on this butte than on the prairie below, with blue gentians and other alpine favorites.

When you puff to the summit you'll find a solar-powered antenna and a 360-degree view. Zumwalt Prairie stretches to the north, a many-fingered mesa bordered by the rimrock-striped canyonlands of the Imnaha River.

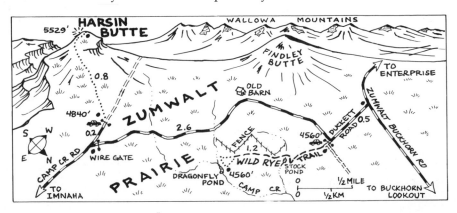

Getting There: From Interstate 84 at La Grande, turn northeast on Highway 82 for 65 miles to Enterprise, and continue 3.2 miles toward Joseph. At a pointer for Buckhorn Spring between mileposts 68 and 69, turn north onto paved Crow Creek Road for 1.1 mile to a fork. Veer right to stay on Crow Creek Road for another 3.9 miles to another fork. Then veer right onto Zumwalt Road, which is paved for the first 2.4 miles.

For Buckhorn Lookout, continue 30 miles across Zumwalt Prairie. At a sign for Buckhorn Overlook (9 miles after Zumwalt Road becomes Forest Road 46), turn right on Road 780. After 0.3 mile go straight at a junction for the primitive, free, 6-site Buckhorn Campground. Keep right at the next two forks to reach the Buckhorn Lookout parking turnaround (GPS location N45 45.232' W116 49.401').

To find the Wildrye Trail, drive back from Buckhorn Lookout on Zumwalt Road toward Enterprise 19 miles. (If you're coming from Enterprise, go out Zumwalt Road until you've driven 11.2 miles of gravel.) At a sign for Duckett Road, turn east on a one-lane gravel road half a mile and park where the road turns sharply right (GPS location N45 33.563' W116 59.052').

For the hike to Harsins Butte, drive Duckett Road south and east another 2.6 miles, open a wire gate (and close it behind you), turn right on gravel Camp Creek Road for 0.2 mile to a cattle guard, and park beside the road (GPS location N4532.149' W11657.383').

Hiking Tips: Pets, horses, fires, vehicles, and camping are banned along Nature Conservancy trails. For the Wildrye Trail, walk straight ahead past a brown metal gate. After half a mile the road/trail switchbacks down past a 30-foot stock pond. Continue 200 yards to the cornerpost of a fenceline. Here the path becomes faint. Continue straight (southeast) 0.4 mile to another fence cornerpost. The path may be lost amid the grass, but continue 200 yards to a (dry) creek swale and follow it left to a pond that makes a good turnaround point (GPS location N45 33.105' W116 57.968').

For the hike up Harsin Butte, walk across the cattle guard and veer left off the road toward the butte. Although there is no trail up this rounded knoll, it's the only hill for miles, so there's not much chance of confusion.

Scramble back down to your car. If you have plenty of gas, you might round out the day by driving back through the hamlet of Imnaha, touring a rough but very wild and beautiful canyon. Drive gravel Camp Creek Road east 11 miles to paved Highway 350. Joseph is 28 miles to your right. Imnaha is a mile to your left.

The country store in Imnaha doesn't sell gas. Painted wooden statues of cigar-store Indians guard the door. Posters invite visitors to an annual rattlesnake feed. And a sign in the window reads, "Hot Beer, Lousy Food, Bad Service. Welcome. Have a Nice Day."

GOING DOWN AT OREGON CAVES

For me, spring is all about breaking winter's cabin fever with some weird outdoor escape. For example, why not hike underground and spend the night in a treehouse?

If you haven't been to the Oregon Caves recently, it's time you got down there. The state's first and tiniest National Monument is one of Southern Oregon's quirkiest getaways.

I'm personally interested in the caves because my grandfather, Austin B. Brownell of Grants Pass, was an electrician who installed wiring there in the 1930s. Family legend says Grandpa was one of the Oregon Cavemen, a strange booster group that dressed in animal skins, carried clubs, and abducted visiting celebrities under the direction of a mysterious Chief Bighorn.

You may laugh, but the Cavemen managed to induct four U.S. presi-

The Oregon Cavemen, a Grants Pass booster group (1940s photo courtesy OCNM).

Cavemen on Guard at the Portals of the Oregon Caves.

dents as members. A 30-foot caveman statue still hefts his club by the Grants Pass exit on Interstate 5.

I'll tell you more about the caves in a minute. But first, you may well be wondering where to stay while you're in this neck of the woods. The Oregon Caves' grand old lodge, the 1934 Chateau, opens in May, so it's the logical first choice. Nearby campgrounds also open in May.

But if you're trying to be adventurous, you might try hanging out at the Treesort. Near Takilma, this private forest offers ten rentable treehouses. Lodgings are connected by stairs, cable ziplines, and swinging footbridges as much as 40 feet in the air.

Accommodations in the trees are actually pretty posh, with queen-size beds. A few of the aerial yurts, tepees, and cabins actually have plumbing and claw-foot tubs. The rest have access to a ground cabin with a bathroom, a kitchen, and a Foosball table.

Michael Garnier, owner and builder of the tree-themed resort, started his career as a physician's assistant in the Midwest. He moved to this hippie-centric corner of Oregon

"Paradise Lost" in the caves.

in the 1970s, built a treehouse for his children, and enjoyed it so much that he started building treehouses for adults too.

To complete his tree resort, Garnier added a 50-foot swing and over ten ziplines—cables strung from tree to tree. Dangling from a pulley with a safety strap and a helmet, you can zing a mile through the woods on the ziplines to end up at your treehouse cabin.

The treehouses have been designed to withstand a lot of weight and stress, but some are closed during windstorms, so check before you go.

Now, about the caves. They're cool. In fact, they're 42 degrees Fahrenheit all year, so you'll need to bring warm clothes. You won't need flashlights, though, and you're not allowed to bring backpacks.

The ranger-guided, 90-minute cave tour climbs 0.6 mile up staircases and through passageways. Along the way you pass marble caverns with stalactites, pillars, and other dripstone formations that you won't see in other Northwest caves.

If you haven't been here for a while, you'll notice that the caves have a more natural look, thanks to a 14-year, $1.2-million restoration effort.

Workers removed a thousand tons of rubble left by earlier construction projects. Bats have been allowed to return. Some of the stalactites broken

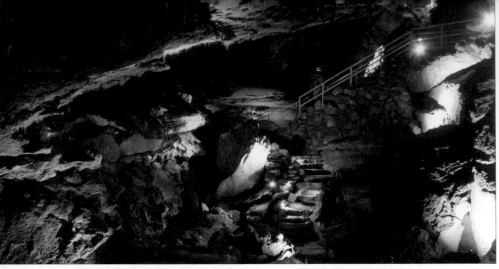

The Ghost Room (photo courtesy Oregon Caves National Monument).

off as souvenirs by early visitors have been repaired with epoxy and powdered marble.

Bright colored lights have been replaced by a subtler incandescent lighting system, lessening the algae growth that had started to turn the marble green. Paths of native quartz and calcite have taken the place of asphalt.

The tours now also showcase animal bones discovered during the restoration project, including grizzly bear bones more than 50,000 years old. Other bones found in the cave belonged to black bears, a bobcat, bats, small rodents, and two jaguars—a mammal that has been extinct in Oregon for millennia.

Children under six must be at least 42 inches tall to join the standard cave tours, although rangers offer some tours for families with kids. Another option is an adventurous off-trail tour, where rangers take serious spelunkers into parts of the cave that are usually off limits. On an off-trail tour, lit only by headlamps, you could easily imagine you're discovering these great Marble Halls for the first time.

The Oregon Caves were not discovered all that long ago. People had been living in Oregon for more than 14,000 years before someone finally stumbled across the entrance.

Elijah Jones Davidson, the cave's discoverer, was born in Illinois in 1849. His family brought him to Oregon in a covered wagon as a baby. They homesteaded in what is now southeast Portland for a few years, moved to a Willamette Valley farm near Monmouth for a decade, and then moved to Williams, a settlement 15 miles south of Grants Pass.

In 1874 Davidson shot and wounded a deer while hunting in the remote, forested hills half a dozen miles south of Williams. His dog Bruno helped him track it down a hillside. There he saw a bear vanish into a cave.

According to an account Davidson published years later, he and his dog gave chase to the bear. He lit matches to find his way through narrow passageways. When his last match died he managed to find his way out by crawling on the cave floor down a streambed until the water led outside.

Frustrated that he hadn't caught the bear, Davidson tracked down the deer, killed it, and left the carcass outside the cave as bait. He bagged the bear later, after it had come out, eaten its fill, and fallen asleep.

Word of Davidson's cave spread slowly at first. In 1885 entrepreneur Walter Burch hired a crew to build a trail to the cave and install wooden ladders inside. He distributed posters advertising the "Grandest Discovery of the Age." Virtually no one came, so Burch gave up in 1888.

Before long a new set developers, led by Alfonso Smith of San Diego, managed to get articles about the "Oregon caves" published in the San Francisco Examiner. Smith boasted to reporters, outrageously, that the caves had 22 miles of passageways and 600 chambers. A horse and buggy, he lied, could be driven ten miles inside. The excitement ended in 1894, when Smith vanished and the promoters' investment company collapsed.

Joaquin Miller toured the caves in August of 1907. One of the most popular American writers of the age, the flamboyant "Poet of the Sierras" had grown up in Lane County near Coburg.

Miller's articles about the Oregon Caves drew a national audience. He railed that the unprotected "great Marble Halls of Oregon" had been vandalized by visitors breaking off stalactites.

Miller thundered that the site deserved National Monument status. Bowing to the need for preservation, President William H. Taft proclaimed a 480-acre National Monument on July 12, 1909.

Getting There: From Interstate 5 at Grants Pass, drive Highway 199 southwest 32 miles to Cave Junction. Turn left, following "Oregon Caves" pointers on Highway 46 for 20 miles to a parking turnaround. Then walk the road ahead 0.2 mile to the gift shop, visitor center, and cave entrance.

Travel Tips: Cave tours are offered only from late March through November. Tickets are sold only at the National Monument and only on a first-come-first-served basis. Pets are banned on National Monument trails. For reservations and directions to the Treesort, check *www.treehouses.com* or call 541-592-2208.

So far, more than three miles of passageways have been discovered.

There's still plenty of room here for adventure—and a chance for a great escape from winter's cabin fever.

15

EMERGING AT TAMOLITCH POOL

Of course the McKenzie River is magical. Almost everyone who loves this river knows that it emerges fully grown from Clear Lake, a pool with a ghostly underwater forest of 3000-year-old snags. Even casual visitors have seen where the river tumbles over Sahalie Falls, a cataract named for the Northwest Indians' spirit world.

But not everyone knows that the river also goes underground for three miles, and that it emerges at turquoise Tamolitch Pool at the foot of an eerily dry, phantom "waterfall."

And although most travelers have heard of Belknap Hot Springs' swimming pool, how many know about the free, natural hot springs just five miles up the riverbank trail?

The McKenzie River Trail passes all these wonders on its 26.5-mile route from McKenzie Bridge to Clear Lake. The path is popular with mountain bikers as

well as hikers. No parking permits are required at the trailheads—in fact, you don't need a car at all, because the Lane Transit District runs regular buses from Eugene to the trailhead at the McKenzie Bridge ranger station.

Start at the ranger station if you're planning a serious hike or a moderate bike ride. Walk across the highway from the parking lot's west entrance, take an obvious but unsigned trail 50 yards to the riverbank, and turn right on the McKenzie River Trail amid Douglas firs six feet in diameter. This lower portion of the trail is usually snow-free all year.

The first few miles of the trail often detour away from the river, approaching within earshot of the highway. At the 3.2-mile mark you'll reach a picnic table and a log footbridge at Lost Creek. This is a lovely spot for lunch, and a possible turnaround point for hikers.

If you continue another 0.7 mile up the trail you'll cross the paved entrance road to Belknap Hot Springs. The remodeled lodge and its 102-degree riverside swimming pool are 0.2 mile to the left. The pool is open 365 days a year 9am to 9pm, and costs about $7 an hour.

The discordant note here for old-time visitors is that the new owners have intensively

The McKenzie flows underground through lava tubes for 3 miles before emerging at Tamolitch Pool.

The McKenzie River Trail traverses a mossy rainforest below Tamolitch Dry Falls.

landscaped the grounds, replacing the old-growth forest's native shrubs with alien plants, concrete, and statuary.

If you're on a bicycle, you won't have any trouble continuing 5 miles up the river trail to a free soak in a wilder hot springs. When you reach the Deer Creek Road crossing, look for a path from the road's bridge that heads downstream 200 yards to Deer Creek Hot Springs. Only an impromptu dike of river rocks separates this shallow two-person pool from the icy river. Depending on the river level, the little pool can be chilly or hot.

The next geologic curiosity in the area, the dry "waterfall" at Tamolitch Pool, is another 7.2 miles up the trail—a perfectly reasonable goal for mountain bikers, but too far for day hikers. To shorten the walk to a mere 2.1 miles, drive to a closer trailhead on gravel Road 655.

From this quiet, upper trailhead, the first mile of the path is nearly level, through an old-growth forest of Douglas fir and

Getting There: To find the trailhead at the McKenzie Ranger Station, drive 2.2 miles of McKenzie Bridge on Highway 126 or take the bus from Eugene for about $3 round trip. For a trailhead closer to Tamolitch Pool, drive Highway 126 east of McKenzie Bridge 14 miles. Beside the upper end of Trailbridge Reservoir, turn left at a "EWEB Powerhouse" sign, cross a bridge, and promptly turn right on gravel Road 655. At a curve after 0.4 mile, park by hiker-symbol sign on the right.

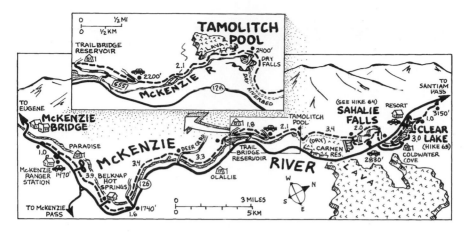

droopy red cedar alongside the rushing whitewater river. Then the trail climbs another mile through a moss-covered lava flow to an overlook of blue-green Tamolitch Pool. The lake's only apparent inlet is a dry waterfall, yet the McKenzie River rages out of the pool at full throttle.

In Chinook jargon, the old trade language of Northwest Indians, *tamolitch* means "bucket". The name fits this cliff-rimmed basin. A gigantic lava flow from Belknap Crater buried three miles of the riverbed here 1600 years ago.

Except during rare floods, the McKenzie was left to percolate underground through lava tubes and porous rock to underwater springs inside Tamolitch Pool. A 1963 hydroelectric project has left the dry stretch of riverbed even drier. The Eugene Water and Electric Board catches the river in Carmen Reservoir, diverts it through a 2-mile tunnel to Smith Reservoir, and drops it through a second tunnel to the Trail Bridge power plant.

Beyond Tamolitch Pool the McKenzie River Trail climbs past Koosah

Falls and Sahalie Falls to Clear Lake—all delightful goals as well, but they are just close enough to the highway that they have become familiar tourist stops. The magical McKenzie River shares its deepest secrets only with those who are willing to go the extra mile.

Left: Deer Creek Hot Springs.
Above: Fairy slipper orchid.

16

WESTERN OREGON HOT SPRINGS

T he best hot springs in Oregon's backwoods have no signs. On a chilly February morning, only a wisp of steam through the trees may mark these hidden spas. Hikers here sport goosebumps, towels, and ruddy glows.

If you're ready to take the plunge, here are the steamy details of Western Oregon's outdoor hot springs, from the crowded to the unvisited. Note that I am leaving out illegal destinations (such as Austin Hot Springs, on private land along the Clackamas River) and hot springs in Eastern Oregon, which I cover on pages 90-95 and 190-195.

The Crowded: McCredie, Terwilliger, and Bagby

Swimsuits are rare at Western Oregon's three most popular soaks. A roadside attraction in "bare country," McCredie Hot Springs' 20-foot-wide pool is just a 100-yard walk from Highway 58. Truck drivers share the free natural spa with longhair spiritualists and apres-ski snowboarders. To

My wife Janell poses at McCredie Hot Springs, a free roadside stop near Oakridge. I posed in the buff at my favorite soak, Umpqua Hot Springs (above), but Janell altered the photo.

The bathhouse at Oregon's most popular soak, Bagby Hot Springs, burned in 1979, but was rebuilt with additional tubs (below).

join in, drive the highway southeast past Oakridge to a sign for "McCredie Sta. Road" near milepost 45 and park in a big unmarked gravel lot on the right.

At Terwilliger Hot Springs (alias Cougar Hot Springs), half a dozen small pools terrace a forest glen overhung by cedars. Crowds and a few police calls here have led the Forest Service to close the area after dark and ban camping within a few miles. What really cleaned up the crowd here, however, was the introduction of a special parking fee at the trailhead. To drive here, take McKenzie Highway 126 east past Blue River, turn right at a sign for Cougar Reservoir, and continue 4 miles past the dam to a collection of cars on the right. Then hike a level, unmarked trail half a mile to the springs.

Bagby Hot Springs, a long-time favorite for Portlanders, is reached by a lovely 1.5-mile stroll through massive old-growth woods on the edge of the Bull of the Woods Wilderness. The only fee required here is the standard Northwest Forest Pass for your car. It's available at the trailhead, or you can pick one up at ranger stations and outdoor stores.

The springs themselves have been channeled through a flume

Belknap Hot Springs pipes hot water across a McKenzie River footbridge to its pool.

past a rustic bathhouse with five free private rooms, each containing an eight-foot-long cedar bathtub carved from a log. The rooms, and a half dozen nearby open-air tubs, are so popular you'll probably have to wait two hours for a turn on summer weekends. On weekday mornings, however, you'll have your choice of tubs. To drive here, take Highway 224 from Oregon City through Estacada and continue straight up the Clackamas River, following signs for Bagby Hot Springs. Don't leave valuables in parked cars! In fact, I'd leave the door unlocked. There are more break-ins at this trailhead than at all other Oregon trailheads combined.

The Commercial: Breitenbush and Belknap

The commercial resorts that sprang up at Breitenbush and Belknap Hot Springs in the late 1800s have evolved in very different ways. At Belknap (described on page 67), the hot springs supply a concrete swimming pool wedged between an upscale lodge and the rushing river. Swimsuits are a must.

At Breitenbush Hot Springs (on Breitenbush Road, 9 miles from the hamlet of Detroit), the resort's original concrete pool has been closed in favor of open-air hot tubs and "sacred pools" where clothing is consensual. The resort itself has become a New Age retreat center with programs on healing arts and self awareness. Check before you go, because the resort is sometimes open only to guests who have signed up for a conference. For information call 503-854-3320 or check *www.breitenbush.com*.

The Tepid: Deer Creek

Several smaller hot springs in the Cascade foothills are too chilly for a proper soak—but the temperature varies. Perhaps the best example is Deer Creek Hot Springs, described on page 68.

The Treat: Umpqua

The last best hot soak in Western Oregon is Umpqua Hot Springs—a 105-degree pool in a rustic shelter overlooking the North Umpqua River. To get there, drive Interstate 5 south to Roseburg exit 124 and follow "Diamond Lake" signs 58.6 miles east on Highway 138. Between mileposts 58 and 59, turn left onto Toketee-Rigdon Road 34. After 0.2 mile keep left alongside Toketee Lake's dam. Continue 2 miles, fork right onto gravel Thorn Prairie Road 3401 for precisely another 2 miles, and look for a huge parking lot on the left.

A trail sets off across the North Umpqua River on a 150-foot bridge. On the far side, take a steep side trail up to the right for 0.2 mile to the shelter. The main pool holds four or five people, but a string of half a dozen similar pools beside the shelter ranges from very hot to warm. Another warm spring down on the riverbank below the shelter is covered by the river during high water.

After soaking a while and hiking back to the parking lot, don't miss a short side trip to two strange cold springs nearby. This trail starts beside the parking lot's outhouse, climbs to the road, follows it 100 feet, and then descends left into the woods. In 0.3 mile you'll reach Surprise Falls, which roars out of the ground just below the trail, and Columnar Falls, where lacy springs spill down a mossy basalt cliff and vanish without a trace.

The original pool at Umpqua Hot Springs is beneath a shelter (above), but many others have been carved into the rock nearby (below).

JUNE
IN OREGON

A cave along the trail over-looks the Deschutes River.

17

SCOUT CAMP TRAIL

For years my favorite Central Oregon escape was Smith Rock, a sure desert retreat for hikers driven out of the Cascades by lousy weather. Whenever my favorite mountain trails were wreathed in rain or buried under snow, I'd get in the car and flee east to the dry beauty of Smith Rock's riverside canyon.

But now I have a new favorite Central Oregon escape: the Scout Camp Trail.

This 3-mile loop descends past cliffs, caves, and wildflowers to a wild stretch of the Deschutes River opposite the confluence of Whychus Creek. This is the same tantalizingly beautiful terrain you can see—but cannot access—from the Whychus Creek Trail to Alder Springs.

The Scout Camp Trail is one of several paths built by the Bureau of Land Management on the fringes of the Crooked River Ranch, a sprawling rural subdivision of vacation homes and ranchettes on the rimrock plateau between the Deschutes and Crooked Rivers.

Many people bought lots here because of Central Oregon's reputation as a recreation center, but the ranch's developers really didn't think to provide much in the way of parkland or public trails. So the BLM has stepped in, partly to stop desperate recreationists from creating dangerous and damaging scramble paths in the rugged canyons bordering the ranch.

The new trails aren't just for locals, although it can seem that way. The only access is through the Crooked River Ranch's labyrinth of mostly paved but weirdly confusing roads.

Open only to hikers, the Scout Camp Trail starts out perfectly level, through viewless, dusty juniper woods with bunchgrass and sagebrush. A few blue larkspurs bloom here in May and June.

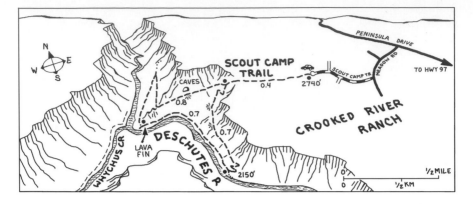

After 0.3 mile the trail begins its descent into the Deschutes' canyon, with views across the rimrock to the Three Sisters. Three Fingered Jack peeks over the left shoulder of Black Butte.

In another 200 yards, fork left at the start of the loop. Now the path switchbacks down bouldery sagebrush slopes brightened with huge clumps of yellow balsamroot sunflowers.

At the bottom of a cliff near the river the trail forks again. Ignore the deadend scramble path to the left, and instead follow the main trail downstream to the right.

This section of the loop is a little rough and rocky, tracing a cliff's base. Lava flows from the Cascades 5 to 25 million years ago left the basalt in these cliffs. Trapped between the rock layers are softer strata of ash, river cobbles, and cooked soil—evidence of the devastation unleashed by the lava flows.

Views extend across the rimrock to the Three Sisters.   Above: Monkeyflower.

The trail passes turbulent rapids where Whychus Creek joins the Deschutes River.

At the 1.8-mile mark the trail appears to deadend at a wall where a lava fin juts into the river. To continue you have to use your hands to climb 8 feet up and over the lava wall, 30 feet before the path reaches the river. It's not difficult, but it's also not obvious.

Beyond the lava fin the path climbs 0.4 mile to a junction. Ignore the scramble path straight ahead (which soon peters out), and instead switchback up to the right. Now you'll climb to a ridge and hike past several shallow caves, where soft ash flow deposits have eroded out below the basalt rimrock.

Keep left to complete the loop. Back at your car you can decide whether you, too, have discovered a new favorite hike in Central Oregon.

Getting There: Drive Highway 97 just north Terrebonne (6 miles north of Redmond or 20 miles south of Madras) to a pointer for the Crooked River Ranch and turn west on Lower Bridge Road for 2.1 miles. Then, watching your odometer carefully, turn right on 43rd Street for 1.8 miles, turn left on Chinook Drive for 2.4 miles, turn left on Mustang Road for 1.1 mile, turn right on Shad Road for 1.4 miles, turn right on Peninsula Drive for 3.3 miles, turn left on Meadow Road for 0.6 mile, and turn right on gravel Scout Camp Trail a quarter mile to the trailhead at road's end (GPS location N44 27.663' W121 19.294').

DOG MOUNTAIN

C an't wait to hike amid the alpine wildflower meadows of summer? At Dog Mountain, entire hillsides of spectacular summer flowers are blooming a full two months ahead of popular flower fields in the High Cascades.

The secret of Dog Mountain is its location, on the Washington side of the Columbia River an hour's drive east of Portland. By June, and often even by May, warm breezes from Eastern Oregon have teased a whole palette of colors from the alp-like slopes here, including yellow balsamroot, red paintbrush, and blue lupine. Views from the summit meadows extend up and down the Columbia Gorge to cliffs spouting waterfalls.

Such beauty has made the steep climb popular, but the mountain has three different trails to the top, so you can take your pick. Don't be tempted by the Old Trail, even though it is the shortest. Originally built for pack horses en route to a (now abandoned) lookout tower site, the Old Trail charges straight up the mountain through deep woods.

The newest path here, the Augspurger Mountain Trail, spirals up Dog Mountain as gently as a railroad grade. But it's the longest route and misses most of the views.

The best choice if you're looking

Wild onions (below) are among the many flowers that bloom in the meadows (above).

for wildflowers is to head uphill on the steepish but scenic Dog Mountain Trail. Then you can return on the gentler Augspurger Mountain Trail to complete a loop that's easy on the knees.

Getting There: From Portland, drive Interstate 84 to Cascade Locks exit 44, take the Bridge of the Gods across the river (paying a $1 toll on the way), and turn right on Washington Highway 14 for 12 miles. Between mileposts 53 and 54, at a sign fo the Dog Mountain Trailhead, park in a huge pullout on the left.

So start out from the far, right-hand end of the parking lot. This path begins along an ancient road but after 100 yards turns sharply left and begins a relentless, switchbacking climb. Beware of lush, three-leaved poison oak along these lower slopes. Also notice early summer wildflowers: baby blue eyes, lupine, yellow desert parsley, and purple cluster lilies on onion-like stalks.

After half a mile the trail forks. Ignore the left-hand path—the precipitous, viewless Old Trail. Instead turn right, through a Douglas fir forest brightened in spring by big three-petaled trilliums and tiny six- or seven-petaled starflowers. This path climbs almost a mile before suddenly emerging at a viewpoint on a windswept, grassy knoll. In early summer, sunflower-like balsamroot and red paintbrush spangle this pleasant picnic spot—a satisfactory turnaround point for a moderate hike. The view extends across the chasm of the Columbia Gorge to Starvation Creek Falls and sometimes-snowy Mt. Defiance.

The 186-foot waterfall visible across the river on Starvation Creek earned its name during an 1884 blizzard, when thirty-foot snowdrifts there marooned two trains making the run through the Columbia Gorge from

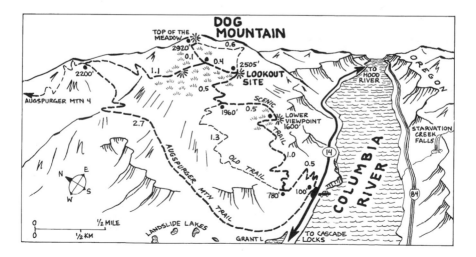

Portland to Hood River. At first the stranded passengers burned the locomotives' coal to keep warm. Then they burned chairs and woodwork. Meanwhile the railroad company dispatched skiers from Hood River with emergency food. Able-bodied passengers were offered three dollars a day to help dig out the track. Finally, after two weeks in the grip of the storm, the trains steamed loose of their wintry trap.

If you still have enough energy after hiking to Dog Mountain's lower viewpoint, climb onward to the grander meadows on Dog Mountain's summit. Continue half a mile to another junction with the Old Trail, and head uphill at a gruelingly steep grade for another half a mile to an old fire lookout site in a steep wildflower meadow. Then take a sharp left turn and keep heading uphill for a final half mile to your destination: the top of the meadow, afloat in panoramic vistas from Hood River to Mt. Hood and Cascade Locks.

Notice the flavorful assortment of wildflowers at this lofty viewpoint — wild strawberry, chocolate lily, and wild onion.

Turn back after soaking in the view from the top of the meadow. (If you keep going, the trail ahead merely dives into viewless woods.) So turn around, hike back down through the meadow 200 yards, and turn right at a sign for Augspurger Mountain. This path descends a ridge with views of its own for 1.1 mile. Then turn left at a junction. For the final 2.7 miles back to your car, the Augspurger Mountain Trail gently arcs halfway around Dog Mountain, like the path of an airplane coming in for a landing — after a flight that offered a sneak preview of summer's flowers.

Dog Mountain from the Oregon side of the river.   *Above: Balsamroot.*

PINE MOUNTAIN'S STARS

Red paintbrush bloom near Pine Mountain's observatory.

The stars shine bright on Pine Mountain, a 6300-foot ridge on the edge of the desert east of Bend. The place is best known for its visitable University of Oregon observatory, but the mountain itself is also a star attraction. With a bit of easy bushwhacking you can hike along the open crest of a rolling ridgeline, discovering rock formations, ponderosa pine groves, wildflowers, and views across Eastern Oregon.

If you plan your visit for a Friday or Saturday, you can hike in the afternoon, eat a picnic dinner at sunset, and spend the evening peering through a telescope at the stars. The University of Oregon uses a 32-inch telescope at Pine Mountain for research, but visitors are allowed to take a look through a 24-inch telescope.

Because the nighttime stargazing often runs late, you might plan to camp across the road from the observatory. Pine Mountain's free, primitive

A rock outcrop on Pine Mountain.

campground is set among pine trees, with picnic tables and an outhouse. Bring all the water you'll need, because there is none here.

When you first arrive at the observatory's parking area, walk up past a locked green gate marked "Quiet Zone". A ten-foot dome to the right houses a 14-inch telescope that's robotically controlled for the use of remote researchers via the Internet.

Continue up the road to a larger silver dome on a white concrete block base. This houses the 24-inch scope. It's big enough to make quite a show of the moons of Jupiter, the rings of Saturn, the nebula of Lyra, and other celestial wonders.

Behind is another large dome with a 32-inch research telescope. All the telescopes have been placed a little below Pine Mountain's summit to avoid high winds that would shake the instruments.

If you're interested in taking a longer hike along Pine Mountain's ridgetop, take a path that starts beside the white concrete-block observatory. This trail climbs 200 yards to a summit where a low stone shelter serves as a windscreen. Views extend to the Three Sisters and Mt.

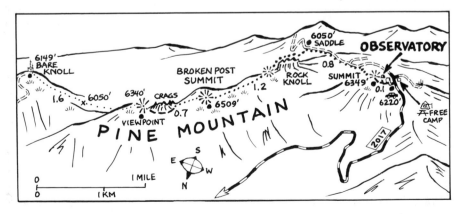

Jefferson. Twelve-petaled, cream-colored bitterroot flowers bloom among the sagebrush in June.

   Long pants, boots, and a sense of adventure are required to bushwhack beyond this point. If you're game, scramble east along the ridge two miles to a summit marked only with a broken wooden post. This is actually the highest point of Pine Mountain, and a possible turnaround spot, but there's a better view in another 0.7 mile.

   Wherever you turn back, make sure you leave enough time to reach your car before dark. Take a flashlight just in case—and bring along a red filter or a red piece of cellophane to put over the flashlight at the observatory.

Bitterroot flowers bloom in June.

   Only red lights are allowed near the telescopes. The red light lets your eyes adjust to the night, so the stars at Pine Mountain seem to blaze all the brighter.

Getting There: Drive Highway 20 east of Bend toward Burns for 26 miles. At milepost 26 you'll pass Millican's closed store. Continue another quarter mile to a big green sign for the Pine Mountain Observatory and turn right on a wide red cinder road. After crossing a cattle guard in another 3.3 miles, veer to the right on one-lane gravel Road 2017, climb 4.7 miles to a saddle, and pull into the observatory parking area on the left (GPS location N43 47.503' W120 56.471').

Tips for Visitors: Volunteers are usually on hand to give observatory tours every Friday and Saturday night from late May through September. Be sure to dress warmly, show up about an hour before sunset, and bring $5 per person. Large groups should call 541-382-8331 to confirm a visit. More information is available at *pmo-sun.uoregon.edu*.

Tips for Hikers: To bushwhack along Pine Mountain, bring long pants, boots, and a sense of adventure. Walk to the summit behind the observatory, continue straight past a small stone circle (due east), descend a steepish sagebrush slope 0.3 mile to a road, and keep left along the road half a mile. Leave the road at a broad forested saddle where the road turns sharply to the right (GPS location N43 47.523' W120 55.537'). Go straight and level on a faint cattle trail amid ponderosa pines. After 200 yards, scramble up to the right around a big rock outcrop. Regain the ridgecrest beyond the rock outcrop, and continue along the crest a mile to the highest point of Pine Mountain, marked by a post.

20

FLORAS LAKE &
BLACKLOCK POINT

Backpackers at Blacklock Point hike from Floras Lake (above right, with windsurfers) along one of Oregon's quietest beaches.

A hot spot for beginning windsurfers and kite boarders, Floras Lake has also become a secret mecca for hikers and backpackers exploring the wildest part of the state's coast.

Quiet trails from Floras Lake lead along forested bluffs and untrod beaches to Blacklock Point, a headland where time seems to have stopped centuries ago.

Floras Lake was the unlikely site of a boomtown in 1910, when developers promised to make this lake a seaport by cutting a canal through the dunes to the ocean. The town vanished when surveys proved the lake is higher than the ocean, so a canal would only drain it.

Today, reliable winds make this shallow, sandy-bottomed lake the Oregon Coast's most popular windsurfing center for beginners. A windsurfing school here rents equipment. Kiteboarders also ply the waters.

By comparison, Oregon's more famous windsurfing zone, the Columbia Gorge, is far less friendly. The Gorge is known for deep, cold water with whitecapped waves. If you make a mistake there, you end up in Washington. At Floras Lake, you can touch bottom in the warm water almost everywhere.

Getting There: Drive Highway 101 south of Bandon 16 miles to milepost 290, turn west on Floras Lake Loop, and follow signs for 2.8 zigzagging miles to Boice Cope Park. At road's end, just after the campground entrance, turn left into a lakeside parking lot. Expect a small day-use fee.

From the parking area at Floras Lake, hike across a footbridge over Floras Lake's outlet (the New River) and keep left on a lakeshore trail. You'll pass a beach full of windsurfers and kite boarders preparing their gear for launch. After half a mile, when the trail peters out in the sand, head right 200 feet through a gap in the grassy foredune to the ocean.

Walk left a mile along the seashore toward Blacklock Point. After half a mile orange bluffs begin rising beside the beach. At the 0.8-mile mark, watch out for waves that smack all the way to the cliffs at high tide. Beyond this squeeze, the beach widens at a forested canyon where a creek sinks into the sand.

Turn inland here. Keep on the left-hand side of the creek to find a path that climbs into the woods. After 200 yards the trail forks — and you'll face a decision.

If you're ready to head home, turn left and keep left for a short loop that returns to Floras Lake's shore. If you'd like to see Blacklock Point, however, turn right. This portion of the Oregon Coast Trail dips to a creek bridge and climbs to a forested plateau. After 0.8 mile, turn right on a path that skirts the bluff's edge. Two short side trails to the right detour to spectacular coastal viewpoints.

In 1.1 mile you'll reach a junction marked with an Oregon Coast Trail post. Turn right toward Blacklock Point. After half a mile the trail passes

backpacking campsites under the headland's last trees.

Campers need to bring water because there is no reliable source near Blacklock Point. Keep left for 100 feet to a trail fork at the start of the headland meadow. If you go straight you'll explore the headland's tip on increasingly precarious paths.

If you fork left you'll switchback down to a beach with sea stacks and giant jumbles of driftwood logs. Once you hit this beach it's hard not to stroll a mile south to the Sixes River, where a stream ripples calf-deep across the strand.

It's true that there is a shorter route to Blacklock Point. This

Blacklock Point, near Cape Blanco, is accessible only by trail.   Opposite: Sea stack.

shortcut is not as scenic but it is open to bicycles. Hikers will need to wear boots because the path always has mud puddles.

To find this trailhead, drive Highway 101 north of Port Orford 7 miles (or south of the Floras Lake turnoff 4 miles). Between mileposts 293 and 294, turn west off Highway 101 at an "Airport" pointer and follow paved Airport Road for 2.9 miles to a parking area at the gated airport entrance. The trail begins to the left of the gate as a barricaded dirt road paralleling the runway through dense shore pine woods. After 0.8 mile keep left at an unmarked junction. Follow "Blacklock Point" arrows at junctions for the next for 1.1 miles, forking twice to the left and once to the right before emerging at the headland's tip.

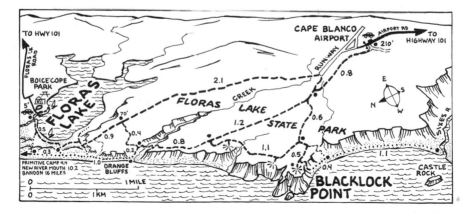

21

HORSEPASTURE MOUNTAIN

Mountain views and wildflower meadows highlight the relatively easy climb to this panoramic former lookout site perched on a crag between the Three Sisters and the McKenzie River Valley.

Horsepasture Mountain was named by early forest rangers. While riding the Olallie Trail from McKenzie Bridge to lookout towers on Olallie Ridge, rangers often camped at Horsepasture Saddle Shelter to let their mounts graze on the nearby peak's meadows. The shelter is gone, but the meadows and views remain.

Indians also visited this area, drawn by the huckleberries that still ripen on Olallie Ridge each August. In fact, *olallie* means "berry" in Chinook jargon, the old trade language of Northwest Indians.

The trail begins amid woodland wildflowers—queens cup, vanilla leaf, bunchberry, and star-flowered solomonseal. After just 80 yards, turn sharply left at a four-way trail junction

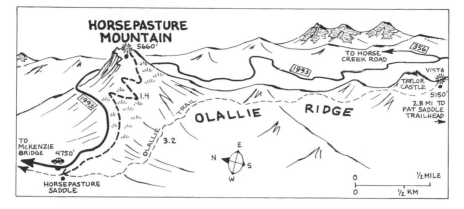

in Horsepasture Saddle. Then you'll traverse Douglas woods for 0.7 mile before entering lush meadows with white beargrass plumes, purple aster, orange tiger lily, columbine, cats ears, and the boat shaped leaves of hellebore. It the trail seems faint at times in the meadow foliage, just keep going onward and upward. The trail's four switchbacks are so clear they're hard to miss.

When you reach the summit's cliff-edge crags, you'll find three large anchor bolts marking the lookout tower's site. The Three Sisters dominate the horizon to the east, with conical Mt. Bachelor to the right and ghostly Mt. Hood far to the left. Below, displayed like a volcanology exhibit, ancient High Cascades lava flows funnel down the great flat-bottomed trough of the McKenzie River Valley toward the blue horizons of the distant Willamette Valley.

The Horsepasture Mountain trail not only has a view of the Three Sisters (upper left), but also columbine (far left), beargrass (below left) and queens cup (above).

Getting There: Drive Highway 126 east of Eugene 50 miles to McKenzie Bridge. Immediately after crossing the village's river bridge, turn right onto paved Horse Creek Road 2638 for 1.7 miles. Just after the Horse Creek Group Campground turn right onto Road 1993, follow this one-lane route for 8.6 winding, uphill miles. Expect fallen rocks and a dozen patches of gravel on the last few miles of this narrow, paved road, so drive slowly. Park at a hiker-symbol sign on the right for the Horsepasture Trailhead.

The Hart of the Desert

Pronghorn antelope streak across the sagebrush slopes of Hart Mountain, a gigantic, tilted plateau edged by a 2400-foot cliff in Southeast Oregon's desert.

A national wildlife refuge has protected the graceful antelope here since 1936. But the area has become a secret refuge for other treasures as well: creeks lined with quaking aspen, a free campground with natural hot springs, views across miles of ephemeral lakes, and mountain slopes ablaze with wildflowers.

Solitude, vast blue skies, and silence seem to stretch forever.

This is a great place to set up a tent near a grassy creekbank, put your feet up on a log, and bask in the early summer sun.

If you like to hike, don't worry. Although there are no marked trails, you don't need them. Good hiking routes simply follow the area's creeks and canyons.

June is perhaps the best month to explore Hart Mountain, after winter's snows have melted and before August's heat wilts the landscape to a dusty brown.

Hart Mountain is a long drive from western Oregon. But it's one of the most beautiful drives in the world. I especially like Highway 31, which passes the old West hamlets of Silver Lake and Paisley. If you need a break on this desert route, stop near milepost 92 for a swim in the rustic 1928 bathhouse of Summer Lake Hot Springs.

Just 5 miles before Lakeview turn left on Highway 140, a lonely paved route built long ago as part of an economic development craze with the slogan, "Winnemucca to the Sea!"

Your next goal is Plush, a tiny ranch settlement with a single store that also serves as the town's cafe, tavern, and gas station. Check your gas gauge here. Then continue slowly, even though the road ahead is paved and pretty much straight. Take time to use binoculars to watch for birdlife in the alkali Warner Lakes. You may also spot bighorn sheep on the cliffy face of Hart Mountain.

The pronghorn antelope on the refuge are North America's swiftest animals, clocking up to 65 miles per hour. They flash their white rumps and release a musk when alarmed to flight. Nearly 2000 live on the refuge, although they often roam south into Nevada.

Biologists long wondered why pronghorns would need to run so fast — more than 20 miles per hour faster than coyotes, mountain lions, or any other North American predator. The fossil record held the answer. Until about 20,000 years ago this area was home to cheetahs. The pronghorns evolved to outrun a predator that is now extinct.

The Barnhardi Basin cabin hides amongst the quaking aspen.   Above: Wild iris.   Lower left: Ancient art at Hart Mountain's Petroglyph Lake.   Above left: Poker Jim Ridge.

Warner Peak from Rock Creek.

A pullout at Hart Lake has a short, overgrown nature trail and a wildlife viewing blind where you ought to see birds, but generally don't.

There's a more interesting roadside stop after the road turns to gravel. Halfway up the long, steep, gravel grade on Poker Jim Ridge, look for a pullout with a hiking trail. This 0.3-mile path loops to a viewpoint across the Warner Lakes far below.

The Ice Age brought rain instead of ice to this area, raising the level of the Warner Lakes 200 feet, uniting them to form an inland sea. You can still see the high-water mark, a smooth band on the side of Poker Jim Ridge. Today all that remains of this former mega-lake is a string of vaguely oval alkali pools, connected by hundreds of sinuous waterways. In spring, when water levels are relatively high, it's fun to explore these lakes by canoe.

After 10 miles of gravel road you'll reach the refuge headquarters, a few buildings with the only tree for miles. The headquarters is often un-

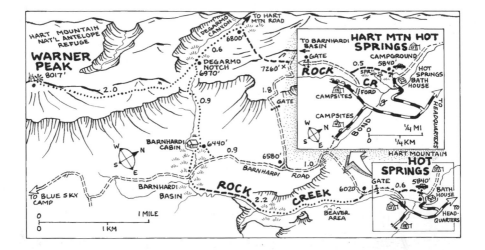

staffed, but a visitor room here is always open, with displays, brochures, restrooms, and the free, self-issuing backcountry permits required for overnighting anywhere except at the Hot Springs Campground.

Beyond the refuge headquarters, keep right at forks for 4.5 miles to a parking area at the hot springs bath house, where a roofless concrete block wall surrounds an 8-by-10-foot rock pool.

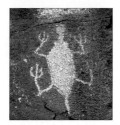

Stop to soak in the free, natural 102-degree pool, watching bubbles rise from the rocks below while songbirds zoom overhead.

Signs note the pool rules: No glass containers. No soap. Maximum stay 20 minutes if others are waiting.

Most visitors take a dip in the hot springs, spend the night in the free campsites along the creeks nearby, and then drive on. But to see the refuge's wildlife and mountain scenery up close, use the campground as a base for some exploration afoot.

For a moderate loop, hike along Rock Creek to an old sheepherder's

Getting There: Drive Highway 97 south of Bend 30 miles (and south of LaPine 2 miles), and fork left on Highway 31 through the old West hamlots of Silver Lake and Paisley for 141 miles. Before Lakeview turn left on Highway 140 for 16 miles to a fork. Following signs for the Hart Mountain Refuge, veer left onto paved Road 3-13 for almost 20 miles to Plush. Continue straight through town 0.8 mile and turn right on Road 3-12 for 24 miles to the Hart Mountain National Antelope Refuge Headquarters. Then keep right at road forks for 4.5 miles to a parking area at the hot springs campground.

Hiking Tips: From the hot springs, cross the parking area from the bathhouse and walk along a closed old road. After 0.2 mile, turn right on Barnhardi Road for 0.3 mile to a silver gate (locked to bar vehicles December 1 to August 1). Continue another 150 yards, but when the road curves to the right away from the creek, fork left on a faint track with a "No Motor Vehicles" sign.

This track soon peters out, but simply continue up Rock Creek for 2.2 miles to Barnhardi Basin, keeping right along the creek's main branch. If Barnhardi Cabin is your goal, you can return on a loop by following Barnhardi Road back to your car at the campground.

If you'd like to climb Warner Peak, skirt the boggy area directly behind the cabin and follow a little creek up through aspen groves 0.9 mile to DeGarmo Notch (GPS location N42 29.094' W119 43.917'). Then traverse uphill to the south, angling below an outcrop of cliffs, to a bare ridge shoulder above a grove of mountain mahogany trees. Continue south along the ridge to Warner Peak's summit (GPS location N42 27.579' W119 44.474'),

cabin at Barnhardi Basin. For a tougher adventure, bushwhack to the area's highest viewpoint, 8017-foot Warner Peak.

Start these hikes by following Hot Springs Creek upstream. The route has no trail, so wear long pants to protect your legs from the sagebrush. Expect to scramble a bit when you pass an aspen grove with trees felled by beaver.

When you reach the broad meadow bowl of Barnhardi Basin, you'll have to cross Barnhardi Road to reach the cabin, a dilapidated 10-by-16-foot plank shack in a grove of giant aspens. If the

OREGON FAVORITES

cabin is your goal, you can return on
a loop by following Barnhardi Road back to your car at the campground.

If you'd like to climb Warner Peak, skirt the boggy area directly behind the cabin and follow a little creek up through aspen groves 0.9 mile to De-Garmo Notch, a broad, grassy saddle.

Then traverse uphill to the south and follow a ridge south. Soon you'll see your goal: a small concrete building and radio towers on the summit of Warner Peak, where views extend from Steens Mountain to California's South Warner Mountains.

For those who have learned to listen to the quiet voice of the high desert, even a lonely summit in the Hart Mountain refuge can be the heart of Oregon.

In wet years, the Warner Lakes grow and connect, as seen here from Hart Mountain. Above left: Paintbrush in Degarmo Canyon.

JULY
IN OREGON

FIVE TRAILS TO
McNEIL POINT

I f I had time for just one last hike at Mt. Hood before I died, I'd head for McNeil Point. Wildflowers, tumbling brooks, and craggy mountain vistas lend alpine splendor to this ridge on Mt. Hood's northwest shoulder. An easy loop circles Bald Mountain to a picture-postcard view of Mt. Hood. But for real alpine drama, continue up to McNeil Point's stone shelter on a high ridge.

I get grief from the Forest Service because I call this hike "McNeil Point" in my guidebooks. The rangers complain that I should label hikes by official trail names, and not by the destination. I do this when I can. But the route to McNeil Point's shelter involves segments of four official trails, and to do it right, you really need to hike 100 yards on an unofficial, nameless trail. I just don't have room in my books to call this the "Top Spur—Pacific Crest—Timberline—Nameless—McNeil Point Trail Hike."

Start on the Top Spur Trail, a short path that climbs through a patch of blue huckleberries (ripe in August) into a forest of mountain hemlock and Douglas fir. Look for bunchberry, carpeting the ground with white blooms in June and red berries in fall.

After half a mile turn right on the Pacific Crest Trail for 60 yards to a big, four-way trail junction that can be confusing. Go uphill to the right on the Timberline Trail. The correct path emerges from the woods after 0.3 mile onto the steep, meadowed face of Bald Mountain, with views

The route to McNeil Point follows portions of five different trails, passing a timberline tarn (at left) and lupines (above) on the way to a stone shelter from the 1930s (at right).

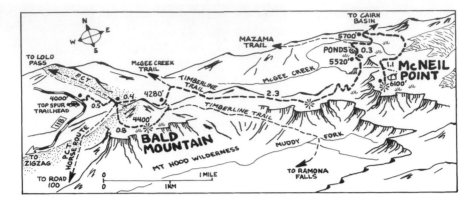

ahead to Mt. Hood and west to the distant Willamette Valley. Stay on the trail to avoid trampling the fragile flowers.

After 0.4 mile through these meadows, watch carefully for the un-signed loop trail around Bald Mountain. This connector crosses a ridge 100 yards to an unsigned junction with another section of the Timberline Trail. For the easy loop, turn left here to return to the car.

If you'd like a longer hike, turn right. On this portion of the Timberline Trail (heading clockwise around Mt. Hood this time), you'll climb up a ridgecrest with wind-dwarfed firs, summer-blooming beargrass, and mountain views. After 1.9 miles the trail switch-backs up a steep wildflower meadow. Then you'll pass a cas-cading, mossy creek and a trail fork at a (sometimes dry) pond amidst a dazzling display of early August wildflowers: red paint-brush, blue lupine, and beargrass. Here sharp eyes can spot the McNeil Point shelter high on the ridge above.

If you're heading for McNeil Point, keep right at junctions, following the Timberline Trail

Take the Timberline Trail around Bald Mountain to find a steep wildflower slope with a full frontal view of Mt. Hood.

another 0.3 mile. Then turn right at a "McNeil Point" pointer and follow a trail up a ridgecrest. The path traverses to the right across a rockslide or snowfield and climbs 1.1 mile to the 10-foot-square stone shelter, built in the 1930s by the Civilian Conservation Corps and later named to honor Portland newspaperman Fred McNeil (1893-1958).

It's legal to camp in here, but it's pretty bleak at night. To protect the scenic dead trees at timberline, campfires aren't allowed within 500 feet of the shelter. When the stars come out, the doorless stone hut becomeis an ice box.

A new path from the Timberline Trail to Mc-Neil Point avoids the old route, a dangerous, damaging scramble up a rock ridge.

My recommendation? Return before it gets dark via the McNeil Point—Timberline—Pacific Crest—Top Spur Trail.

Getting There: Turn north off Highway 26 across from the Zigzag Inn (42 miles east of Portland) onto East Lolo Pass Road. After 4.2 miles fork right onto paved Road 1825. After 0.7 mile, just before a bridge, go straight on unsigned, one-lane paved Road 1828. Continue 5.6 miles and fork to the right on gravel Road 118 for 1.5 miles to the Top Spur Trailhead, with parking on the left (GPS location N45 24.446' W121 47.147').

Hiking Tips: To find the unofficial connector trail around Bald Mountain, hike the Timberline Trail to the right around Bald Mountain. When the trail reenters the woods after the second, smaller meadow, continue 150 steps to a fork in a draw (GPS location N45 24.163' W121 46.242'). If you reach a stock gate to block horses you've gone too far. Take an unmarked left-hand fork over a ridge 100 yards to an unsigned junction with another section of the Timberline Trail. For a short, easy loop, you could turn left here and return to the car. If you're headed for McNeil Point, however, turn right.

Then hike the Timberline Trail to its junction with the McNeil Point Trail (GPS location N45 24.167' W121 43.705') and take this path 1.1 mile to the shelter (GPS location N45 23.727' W121 43.926'). If you're backpacking, be sure to camp out of sight in the woods and not on the fragile meadows. Bring a stove, as campfires are discouraged anywhere near timberline and are banned within 500 feet of the McNeil Point shelter.

LAKELESS IN McCULLY BASIN

It's becoming hard to find a lake in Northeast Oregon's popular Wallowa Mountains where you can be alone. So here's a tip for solitude seekers: Try a beautiful mountain basin *without* a lake.

McCully Basin is just the place for this kind of getaway. Come here if you love alpine brooks, meadows, and high country where you can roam all day without seeing another human. It's also the best base camp for a non-technical climb of Aneroid Mountain, Oregon's ninth tallest peak.

The trailhead to this lonely Eden is a mere 10 miles from the busy tourist town of Joseph.

But crowds continue to overlook McCully Basin because it really doesn't have a lake. No fishing. No swimming.

McCully Basin has no lake, but it has everything else, including two non-technical routes up Aneroid Mountain (above, at the right), Oregon's ninth tallest peak.

If you're OK with that, then a trip here is a reminder of everything else that's wonderful about the Wallowas.

When you start hiking at the McCully Basin Trailhead you'll soon join a gated service road. This dirt track is the route that maintenance vehicles use to drive up to the Wallowa Lake Tramway atop Mount Howard. On the far side of the mountain, the tramway's aerial gondola hoists tourists up from a station near Wallowa Lake Campground for a quick, and expensive, look at the range's high country.

Mountain bikers sometimes take their bikes up the tramway, ride down this service road, and return on a loop through Joseph.

If you're hiking to McCully Basin, follow the service road just 0.7 mile. When the road turns sharply right, fork to the left on an old roadbed that becomes the trail up McCully Creek.

The forest here is mostly lodgepole pine, with Engelmann spruce, Douglas fir, scrub alder, red huckleberry, and blue lupine. You'll also find some pink fireweed, because fires have burned a few patches in these woods.

At the 4.6-mile point the trail crosses 12-foot-wide McCully Creek, a ford that's usually passable dry-footed on rocks. Beyond is the route's first big meadow. This is a possible turnaround point for day hikers.

If you're still going strong, continue 0.6 mile, crossing two small side creeks along the way, to another meadow where you face a choice. Both choices require a sense of adventure. Ahead, the trail suddenly begins to climb. If you charge on ahead for 1.2 miles you'll climb on an increasingly

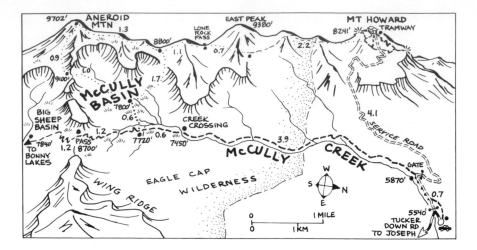

faint trail through increasingly spectacular meadows until you puff to a high pass overlooking Big Sheep Basin and a fair share of the high Wallowas. This is a very nice goal.

If, however, you want to see McCully Basin's main meadows, you'll have to leave the trail and bushwhack 460 feet. This very short off-trail segment is another reason that so few people have discovered the basin's many charms.

Bring a topographic map and a compass. A GPS device will also come

The summit of Aneroid Mountain overlooks Aneroid Lake and the Wallowas.

in handy to keep you on track.

When you bushwhack to the the trailless meadows, Aneroid Mountain looms above a wall of stripey red-brown cliffs on the horizon. A creek burbles out from the field amid purple aster, blue gentian, and white grass of parnassus. The meadows here are heavenly, and even if you come

Sunset from the pass above McCully Basin.

in August you might well be the first visitor of the season.

If you're interested in scaling 9702-foot Aneroid Mountain, plan to set up your base camp in the woods near one of McCully Basin's three meadows. Because there are two non-technical routes to the summit from this side of the peak, it's possible to hike there on a 4.9-mile loop that gains only 1900 feet.

The map shows the general location of these climbing routes, but attempt them only if you also have a detailed contour map and a guide with off-trail experience. Even so, you'll have to use your hands, and there is a danger of rockfall, so helmets are a good idea. Turn back if you're in doubt or if the weather is iffy.

At the top of Aneroid Mountain, an ammo can holds a summit register, but no camera can hold the view. You're at the top of the world, in the heart of the popular Wallowas, and there's no crowd in sight.

Getting There: Drive Interstate 84 to La Grande and turn northeast on Highway 82 for 75 miles to Joseph. At the gas station in the middle of town, turn left off Main Street onto Wallowa Avenue at a sign for Ferguson Ridge. After 5.4 miles, turn right onto Tucker Down Road for 3.1 miles of pavement and another 0.6 miles of good gravel to a ski area parking area. Then continue 1.4 miles on rough gravel (keeping right at junctions) to a turnaround at road's end for the McCully Basin trailhead. If you have a global positioning system (GPS) device, the location here is N45 16.631' W117 08.155'. A Northwest Forest Pass is required to park at the trailhead. Group size on the trail is limited to 12.

Hiking Tips: After 4.6 miles, ford McCully Creek to a meadow. Continue on the trail 0.6 mile until the trail suddenly steepens at a small meadow (GPS location N45 1.03' W117 08.72'). For an off-trail adventure, strike off to the right across the meadow 200 feet, cross a creek, scramble up a sandy slope 60 feet, and continue 200 more feet to the first of McCully Basin's three large meadows (GPS location N45 13.00' W117 08.92').

25

MT. ST. HELENS: RETURN TO GROUND ZERO

W hen Mt. St. Helens unexpectedly aimed its May 18, 1980 eruption sideways, David Johnston, a United States Geological Survey observer, was stationed on a ridge directly in the line of fire. He had time to radio just five words: "Vancouver! Vancouver! This is it!"

Today the most popular drive in the Mt. St. Helens National Volcanic Monument leads to an observation building atop Johnston's ridge. The view of the ruined volcano is both chilling and inspiring. But the panorama actually gets better the farther you hike from the visitor center—it's 1.9 miles to a bluff, 4 miles to Harrys Ridge, and 6.4 miles to Coldwater Peak.

Along the way you'll see how wildflowers and trees have re-populated the volcano-blasted landscape. You'll also see how recent landslides have reopened old wounds on some of the slopes.

Wildflowers and small trees have returned to Johnston Ridge (at left). Stumps remain at the Spillover (above).

In a sense, these fresh landslides are a delayed reaction from the eruption. After about twenty years, the roots of the blast-killed trees finally rotted away, loosening their grip on the soil. Meanwhile, the area's new trees were not yet large enough to anchor the slopes. A similar "delayed reaction" has been credited with causing landslides in Northwest forestland 15 to 20 years after clearcut logging.

The Johnston Ridge Observatory is just a two-hour drive from Portland. It's the last of five visitor centers that once lined the highway up to Mt. St. Helens. Blame the closures on the short attention span of tourists.

You'll need to buy a wrist band at the Johnston Ridge Observatory. It gains you admission to a movie of the mountain's eruption, several exhibits, a large plate glass window overlooking the volcano, and all of the trails outside.

Of course the view is better outside. Just remember that pets are banned outside of the parking area. And be sure to bring plenty of water, because the trails have none.

Start by walking to the observatory's entrance terrace. Then turn left, heading uphill on the paved Eruption Trail, a path that loops across a viewpoint knoll. After 0.3 mile, just before the paved trail returns to the parking lot, turn right onto the unpaved Boundary Trail.

The Boundary Trail ambles east along Johnston Ridge amid splintered logs. Blue lupine and purple penstemon brighten the stark slopes in summer. After half a mile the path dips to the Spillover, a barren saddle where a landslide from the volcano's 1980 eruption sloshed over the top of Johnston Ridge. The massive slide swept away soil and logs, but left behind lava

Getting There: Take Interstate 5 north to Castle Rock exit 49 and turn right onto Highway 504. This paved, 52-mile-long highway dead ends at the Johnston Ridge visitor center.

St. Helens Lake from Coldwater Peak.

boulders. At the 1.9-mile mark, the Boundary Trail switchbacks around the end of a ridge with the best view so far. If you're hiking with children, make this your turnaround point.

For a longer tour, continue 1.5 miles on the Boundary Trail to Harrys Saddle, where the vista opens up across Spirit Lake to distant Mt. Adams. Here you face another choice. For a moderate hike, turn right on a path that climbs 0.6 mile up Harrys Ridge, with its close-up panorama of Mt. St. Helens and Spirit Lake. This ridge was named for Harry Truman, the curmudgeon who died with 40 cats in his Spirit Lake Lodge during the 1980 eruption. Ruined scientific equipment from before the blast remains on the summit.

If you're up for a difficult hike, skip Harrys Ridge and continue straight across Harrys Saddle on the Boundary Trail, heading for the loftier viewpoint atop Coldwater Peak. After climbing 1.7 miles, the path ducks across a ridgecrest through a natural rock arch. Visible far below is blue St. Helens Lake, in a craggy mountain bowl lined with standing dead snags. Continue 0.3 mile down to a trail junction at Arch Saddle, keep right on

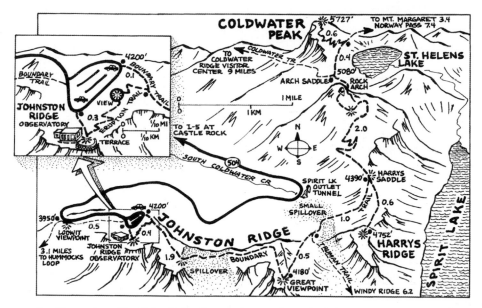

the Boundary Trail for 0.4 mile, and turn sharply left at a sign for the Coldwater Peak Trail.

Patches of snow linger until mid-July on this steep, switchbacking path, but it's also a place to find vibrant alpine wildflowers, including beargrass plumes and pasque flower anemones. Coldwater Peak's summit, once the site of a fire lookout, now has a small collection of antennas and solar panels. The dizzying view extends from Mt. Rainier to the Pacific. But most of the panorama is still recovering from the monumental volcanic blast that overswept Coldwater Peak years ago.

Spirit Lake and Mt. Adams from Harrys Ridge.

26

DANGEROUS ROMANCE AT SALISHAN

June is the perfect month for a romantic walk on the beach, and I've got just the place—the Salishan Spit, as fickle as any beau. This handsome sand peninsula could disappear any day.

At the mouth of the Siletz River at Lincoln City, the peninsula has up-scale beach homes, cheerful sea birds, a colony of 200 comic harbor seals, and a terrifying geologic history.

Like other low areas along Oregon's coast, this spit lies in the path of the next subduction earthquake and tsunami, a catastrophe that's almost certain to occur within the next century or two.

Perhaps you recall the December 2004 Indonesian tsunami, when a quarter of a million people died? Oregon's coast is subject to the same geologic stresses.

One thing that alerted geologists to the danger here was a row of ancient tree stumps at Lincoln Beach, just south of Salishan's ritzy resort. In winter, when storms wash away much of the beach sand, the gnarled roots of long-dead cedar forests lie exposed at Lincoln Beach and many other Northwest beaches.

How could such trees have grown in saltwater, below the high tide line? I remember asking this question as a child. My grandfather shook his head and said, "We don't know. No one knows. This is the Ghost Forest."

In the 1980s, scientists finally got around to analyzing the

Ghost Forest. By comparing the widths of growth rings of living trees, they determined that the beaches' mysterious trees had all died in the same year, 1700.

Something terrible must have happened that year.

Other research brought to light a legend among Washington's coastal tribes that the ground had shaken on a winter night long ago.

A walk out Salishan's sand peninsula (above left) can start at the resort's Nature Trail (below left), pass homes in the dunes (above), and return along the bay's mudflats (below).

Next the investigation turned to Japan, an island nation so plagued by tsunamis that records have been kept for a millennium. Japanese historians reported that a devastating wave had indeed rolled in off the Pacific without warning on the morning of January 27, 1700. Knowing that such waves travel at 500 miles an hour across the Pacific, and having already identified the likely epicenter as a fault zone fifty miles off the Oregon Coast, researchers were able to pinpoint the time of that winter night long ago when the Northwest's shore shook.

The quake that lowered the beach and launched the tsunami struck Oregon at 9pm on January 26, 1700.

As you take your romantic stroll along Salishan's beach, picture the effect such an earthquake would have today. Measuring about nine on the Richter scale, the initial shock would be roughly ten times more powerful than the earthquake that destroyed San Francisco in 1906.

Here at Lincoln City, the ground might suddenly drop ten feet, cracking streets and buildings. Surprisingly, the ocean would not surge forward at once. The waters might even retreat for several minutes, exposing first the tidepools at Fishing Rock, and then the mudflats beyond. By that time sirens would already be wailing in Lincoln City streets,

warning residents to move to higher ground.

Lincoln City is one of the towns on the Pacific shore that has practiced tsunami evacuation drills. Unfortunately, past test runs have sent as many people rushing toward the beach as away from danger. When asked, the curiosity seekers who crowd the shore during tsunami drills say they would like to see a tidal wave first hand.

In the movies, tsunamis are often depicted as towering walls of water 100 feet high. In fact, tsunamis at sea are less than three feet tall — but they are also 100 miles wide. Fishing boats don't even notice them passing by. As the wave nears land it bunches up into a swell that's ten miles wide and as much as twenty feet tall. On the shore, the first breakers can seem small, but they build on one another. It might take several minutes before they sweep away the buildings on Salishan's peninsula.

The blame for these repeated earthquakes lies in our continent's restlessness. North America is charging westward over the Pacific seafloor plate at an average rate of an inch a year. But the movement is not smooth. Because the juncture is sticky, pressure builds up. The coastline arches slightly. Then, every five hundred years or so, the joint suddenly slips, without warning, and the coast springs forward 30 feet. The earthquake can also lower or raise the ground permanently as much as 40 feet.

Because more than three centuries have passed since the last quake, the odds of another are rising.

Nonetheless, I'm not kidding about this sandy peninsula being a great hike. The beach is open to the public, and is almost always empty. Perhaps the most fun part of the hike is ogling the elaborate and often weird homes built by the well-to-do on a foundation of sand that's doomed to shift.

As you hike along this beach the horizon ahead is dominated by the dark green cape of Cascade Head and the Inn at Spanish Head, a 10-story concrete-and-glass bookshelf leaning against the cliffs of Lincoln City. Nestled in the beach dunes are the daring, angled rooflines of Salishan

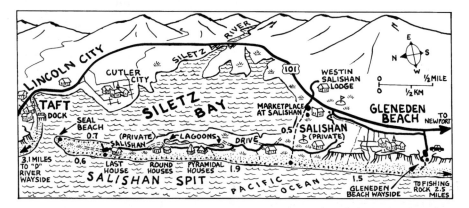

Don't disturb the harbor seals resting at the tip of Salishan's spit.

homes, seemingly clipped from 1960s *Sunset* articles. Pass a pair of pyramidal palaces and then a duo of round domiciles. At the end of the spit, opposite the Taft dock, you'll find 200 or so harbor seals lounging by the bay. Disturbing them is illegal, so don't venture too near.

Continue around the bayshore half a mile until the beach turns to mud. Then turn right across driftwood to the end of paved Salishan Drive. If you're a guest at the resort, you can return on a loop along this private road, rather than merely on the public beach. If you take the road, you'll pass lagoons and picturesquely placed houses for 1.9 miles. When you reach the golf course, either turn left on the nature trail to the Marketplace at Salishan, or turn right on a path to the beach.

If you make it back to the Shops at Salishan, consider stopping for coffee or ice cream. You've earned it, dodging the odds of a tsunami.

Getting There: If you are staying at the Salishan resort, or if you are a guest of a Salishan homeowner, you can start your hike at the Shops at Salishan, 3 miles south of Lincoln City on Highway 101 (near milepost 122). Park at the spa and follow a private nature trail along the dike separating the golf course from Siletz Bay. In half a mile the path crosses Salishan Drive to the beach.

If you don't have connections at Salishan you should start a bit farther away, at the public beach access in Gleneden Beach. To find it, drive 0.8 mile south of Salishan, turn west onto Wessler Street at a sign for Gleneden Beach State Park, and drive 0.2 mile to a huge parking lot and small picnic area. Walk to the beach and head right.

EYE OF THE STORM AT CANYON CREEK

Many hikers have shied from the Mount Jefferson Wilderness since the B & B fire burned a third of the area in 2003. Yes, most of the trailheads here are surrounded by silver snags. But most of the lakeshores and mountain destinations are still green.

Especially at Canyon Creek, you can hike through the burn to an oasis of trees and wildflowers.

The 4.5-mile loop trail to Canyon Creek Meadows is one of the easiest routes to the High Cascades' wildflower meadows. More energetic hikers can continue up a steep glacial moraine to an upper meadow and a breathtaking view of an ice-filled cirque lake beneath Three Fingered Jack's summit pinnacles.

Patches of snow usually block the trail to the lower meadow until the third week of July. The upper meadow has snow until August.

Mosquitoes are not as big a problem

Beargrass is one of many plants that need fire to thrive.

here as at many other Cascades meadows, but they do seem to peak at the same time as the wildflowers, in the last week of July.

The cliffs surrounding Canyon Creek Meadows acted as a natural fire-break in 2003, keeping out the flames. Even where the trees burned—at the trailhead and along the first mile of trail—it's interesting to see how well the forest is recovering.

The lodgepole pine forest in this part of the Cascades has a natural fire cycle of about 100 years. This is why most trees in a stand of lodgepole pine are exactly the same age. It also explains why you seldom see lodgepole pines more than a century old.

The pines have evolved to do well with fires that burn pretty much every tree in a forest. Because lodgepole pines are better at reseeding than other kinds of trees in this zone, fire is a way for the lodgepoles to wipe out competition. Already, millions of lodgepole seedlings have sprouted here on their own.

Other plants also seem to need fire. Beargrass, for example, doesn't bloom in dark woods. After the 2003 fire, beargrass plants resprouted from their roots. The second summer after the fire, they bloomed en masse. They had been waiting 100 years for the trees to burn so they could get enough light to put out seeds.

Similarly, there would be no huckleberry harvest in the High

A 2003 wildfire left snags at Santiam Pass (above), but Three Fingered Jack's cliffs kept the fire from Canyon Creek Meadows (at left).

Cascades if it weren't for fire. If you've hunted berries, you've probably learned that the plants in dark forests have leaves, but no berries. You'll find berries only in old burns, clearcuts, or roadcuts where there's more light.

Huckleberry plants in the deep woods are willing to wait a century for a fire. Then they can finally put out fruit and reseed. Fire has been renewing this forest every century or so since the Ice Age.

To limit the number of people you meet on the trail to Canyon Creek, the Forest Service asks that you hike the loop clockwise. So bear left at the first junction to the lower meadow.

Here the view of Three Fingered Jack's snow-clad crags emerges and the wildflower displays begin in earnest. Do not trample these delicate alpine gardens. Stay on the main trail and choose a picnic spot amid trees. Backpackers must camp at least 100 feet from trails or water.

The cirque lake's milky green color proves that a glacier is still active at Three Fingered Jack, slowly grinding rock to a fine silt.

If you still have plenty of energy, continue 0.7 mile up the trail to the rim of the rock-strewn upper meadow—actually a glacial outwash plain. From here the area's best viewpoint is still 0.8 mile away, and the route

OREGON FAVORITES

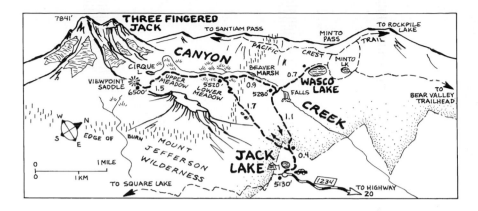

becomes less distinct. Climb south (to the left) up a steep, rocky moraine to a notch overlooking a stunning, green cirque lake at the foot of Three Fingered Jack's glacier. Next the path follows the somewhat precarious crest of the moraine, scrambling steeply up to a windy saddle, where the view stretches from Mt. Jefferson to the Three Sisters. Sharp eyes can often spot climbers on the spires of Three Fingered Jack.

To return via the loop, hike back to the bottom of the lower meadow and turn left. This path follows Canyon Creek past a beaver workshop, where dozens of large pines have been ringed and felled. Rings 6 feet above the ground prove the beavers are active even when snowdrifts remain.

Half a mile beyond the marsh you'll join the trail from Wasco Lake. Just after turning right to return to your car, look left below the trail to spot the first of Canyon Creek Falls' two lovely, 12-foot cascades.

It's hard not to mourn when forests burn at favorite High Cascades destinations. It helps to take the long-range view of forest ecologists. In these woods, fire is a natural process. It's just that the life cycle of the forest is longer than ours.

Getting There: Drive Highway 20 east of Santiam Pass 8 miles. At a "Wilderness Trailheads" sign near milepost 88 (1 mile east of Suttle Lake or 12 miles west of Sisters), turn north for 4.4 miles on paved Jack Lake Road 12. Then turn left on one-lane Road 1230 for 1.6 miles to the end of pavement. Finally turn left onto gravel Road 1234, climbing 6 miles to the trailhead at the primitive Jack Lake campground.

Hiking Tips: Start on the trail to the right, skirting Jack Lake's shore through the burned woods. This path climbs to the wilderness boundary and a well-marked fork at the 0.3-mile point: the start of the loop. Bear left to the lower meadow.

Eagle Creek: The Wallowas' Back Door

I've often wondered why most visitors to the Wallowa Mountains approach this range from the wrong direction.

The Wallowas are a spectacular alp-like chain in northeastern Oregon. Most visitors join the crowds knocking on the range's crowded front door, Wallowa Lake.

The massive state park at Wallowa Lake resembles a small city. The overused trails there are churned to dust.

It's much nicer to slip into the scenic Wallowa Mountains by their less used "back door," along Eagle Creek.

The Ice Age glaciers that scalloped the southern Wallowa Mountains left granite lake basins mounted around the rim of Eagle Creek's spectacular valley. The basins are arranged around the valley like wondrous cupboards in a giant's kitchen.

If you're day hiking you'll have time to peek behind one of those cupboard doors. If you're backpacking, you can visit one alpine lake after another on a grand loop.

The scenery is every bit as dramatic as at Wallowa Lake, but a lack of commercial tourist development has kept Eagle Creek obscure. A landslide obliterated the old Boulder Park Resort that once was the trailhead for hikes here. Today the Boulder Park name lives on as a modest Forest Service campground with ten sites and a horse unloading ramp.

The easiest hiking destination is Eagle Creek Meadow, a creekside field surrounded by granite canyon walls reminiscent of the Swiss Alps. The meadow is 4.4 miles from the trailhead and only 1250 feet up. Elsewhere in the Wallowas, similar hiking goals demand 2000 or 3000 feet of elevation gain.

From a backpacking base camp at Eagle Creek Meadow you can explore the canyon's "cupboards"—the hanging valleys of Bear Lake, Cached Lake, or Arrow Lake. Most of the lakes in the southern Wallowas were dammed long ago to serve as irrigation reservoirs, but these three

If you set up a base camp near Eagle Creek Meadow (opposite page), you can plan day hikes to lakes in nearby hanging valleys, such as Eagle Lake (below).

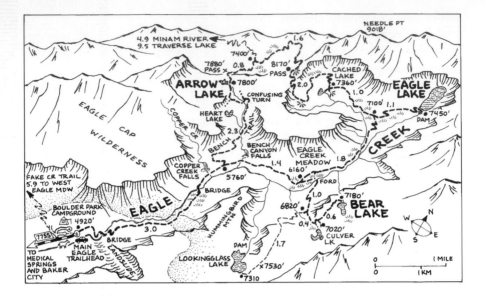

alpine pools remain pristine.

From the trailhead beside the Boulder Park Campground the trail sets off across the debris of the landslide that wiped out the old resort. A white scar on the opposite canyon wall shows where the rock avalanche began.

After crossing scenic footbridges over Eagle Creek at the 0.6-mile and 2.5-mile marks, you'll have to hop on rocks across Copper Creek. Look for the 60-foot fan of Copper Creek Falls to the left.

Gentians open only in full sun.

Continue on the main trail past the 8-foot waterfall of Bench Canyon Creek and hike another mile to the start of Eagle Creek Meadow's vast opening. Where the trail enters the clearing you'll cross an exceptionally well preserved example of glacial polish.

Ice Age glaciers smoothed the bedrock granite here as they ground past 6000 years ago, and the shiny finish still gleams as if wet.

At a well-marked fork, veer right on the Bear Lake Trail into the grassy flat of Eagle Creek Meadow. If you're backpacking, don't camp on top of the fragile meadow plants, but rather among the trees at the far end.

Once you're at Eagle Creek Meadow, you have lots of options for exploring. If you're headed for Bear Lake, wade across Eagle Creek and take a trail 2 miles uphill. A substantial fir forest abuts Bear Lake on three sides, but the far end opens onto a large meadow with a colossal backdrop of cliffs. There's plenty of room to camp on the sparsely wooded rise overlooking Eagle Creek's canyon.

Another popular goal from Eagle Creek Meadow is Eagle Lake, in a stark granite basin at timberline. An ancient dam of hand-fitted rocks is still used to store irrigation water in Eagle Lake.

Perhaps the grandest trip from Eagle Creek Meadow is a 10.9-mile loop past Cached Lake and Arrow Lake. Most of the route is for hikers only, because parts are too rough for horses.

The loop passes through the same kind of high, open alpine country that draws crowds to the Wallowa Lake area.

But because this area is accessed via Eagle Creek, the Wallowas' back door, solitude reigns.

Arrow Lake is on a side trail from the Eagle Creek valley that's suitable only for hikers because it's too rough for horses.

Getting There: From Baker City, take Interstate 84 north 6 miles to exit 298 and drive 19 miles on Highway 203 to Medical Springs, an old stagecoach stop. At Medical Springs turn east on Eagle Creek Drive, following the first of many signs for Boulder Park. The road soon becomes gravel. After 1.6 miles, fork left onto one-lane Big Creek Road 67. After another 14.6 miles, turn left on Road 77 for 0.8 mile and then keep straight on Road 7755 for 3.7 miles to its end at the Main Eagle Trailhead. A Northwest Forest Pass for your car is the only permit you'll need here, and it's available at the trailhead..

Backcountry Tips: The maximum group size in the wilderness here is 12 people. Campsites must be at least 100 feet from any lakeshore, tethered horses must be at least 100 feet from water or campsites, and fires are strongly discouraged. Firewood may only be gathered from downed, dead trees.

AUGUST
In Oregon

29 RETREAT OF THE GLACIERS

What will climate change mean for Oregon? Global warming is a complicated issue, but scientists increasingly agree that long-term changes are coming our way.

Those who enjoy the outdoors may already have noticed ominous trends: Hotter, drier summers. Wetter, warmer winters. Fewer fish. And shrinking glaciers.

When I was a child I remember the Collier Glacier was a river of ice, extending more than a mile between North and Middle Sister almost to a viewpoint on the trail. Now the glacier is hardly half a mile long, and the trail overlooks a gravel field. Similar glacial shrinkage is visible from trails at Mt. Hood and Mt. Jefferson.

At the Three Sisters, you can see the dramatic change by hiking the Obsidian Trail from the McKenzie Pass Highway.

The trail to the Collier Glacier viewpoint is not an easy hike. The path is open only from mid-July through October, and special permits must be

The ongoing melting of Mt. Hood's Eliot Glacier (below, in a photo by Paul Scurlock courtesy of the Mazamas) releases floods of slush and mud that have closed the Timberline Trail for years at a time.   At left: Mt. Hood from Barrett Spur.

The Collier Glacier at the Three Sisters extended 2 miles in 1901. (Photo by Fred Kiser, courtesy of the Mazamas.)

obtained in advance from the ranger station in McKenzie Bridge. Then the walk is 15 miles round trip.

When you reach the viewpoint, you'll notice a "high water mark" on the side of North Sister—a line where lighter rock shows the height of the Collier Glacier a century ago.

The Collier Glacier was once the largest glacier in Oregon. Now that the glacier has lost about 80 percent of its volume, the championship title has shifted to South Sister's Prouty Glacier.

The shrinking of Oregon glaciers is being tracked by the Mazamas, the state's largest outdoor recreation group. The Portland-based club was founded in 1894 when 155 men and 38 women convened in inclement weather on the summit of Mt. Hood. To this day, climbing a glaciated peak is a requirement of club membership.

Photo surveys sponsored by the Mazamas reveal that the state's glaciers have lost much of their volume in the past century. The dwindling ice supply has cut summer streamflows, hurting farmers and fish. Most of the summer irrigation water for Hood River Valley's fruit orchards, for example, comes from Mt. Hood's glaciers.

Oregon's warming climate is changing the types of plants that can grow here. Recent maps prepared by universities for gardeners reflect this new

Oregon Favorites

By 1990 the Collier Glacier had retreated to a half-mile patch of ice on Middle Sister, leaving a gray "high water mark" on the side of North Sister to show its earlier extent.

situation, shifting climate zones north across the continent. Some plants are able to move their range. Other species can't, and become extinct.

In general, the rapid climate shift seems to favor non-native species that are accidentally introduced as weeds. A U.N. climate change panel predicts that about a quarter of all species on Earth will become extinct if temperatures continue to rise in the next few decades.

As Oregon's forestland becomes hotter and drier, Douglas fir may give way to pine. Areas that are now pine may have no forest at all. Oregon's forests will look more like the chapparal of California, and California could resemble Baja California, a cactus desert.

Agriculture is at risk. Oregon has more ghost towns than any other state in the Union. Many of these abandoned villages date to the home-steading era of the early 1900s, when drought devastated farmers, especially in eastern Oregon. As the climate continues to warm, farming in Oregon could again become a precarious occupation.

Oregon's seacoast is also jeopardized. The U.N. panel on climate change anticipates sea levels will rise at least a foot by 2100, but the rise could be as much as 25 feet if the ice caps on Greenland and Antarctica continue to melt rapidly.

At the same time, warmer oceans are creating more powerful storms with larger waves. The average height of waves off the Oregon Coast has been growing by more than a foot a decade. Together, the two trends spell trouble. Low areas will be permanently inundated. Giant storm waves will crumble beach cliffs and wash into coastal communities.

A strange "dead zone" off the Oregon Coast in recent summers appears also to be a result of the changing climate. Oxygen-poor water from the deep ocean wells up offshore, suffocating fish, crabs, starfish, and other marine wildlife. Fishermen say they've heard of fish-free zones for years, but scientists say the problem seems new.

Average temperatures in the Northwest are rising 50 percent faster than in the rest of the world, a panel of eleven independent scientists reported to the Northwest Power Planning Council. Oregon's climate has warmed nearly two degrees Fahrenheit in the past century, and is expected to gain another degree every decade. By the year 2090 almost half of Oregon's rivers will be too hot for salmon to survive.

The Coe Glacier covered the north face of Mt. Hood with ice in 1910. (Photo by Harry Fielding, courtesy of the Mazamas.)

Computer models suggest the melting of the Arctic ice pack will change currents in the Pacific, directing warm, wet winter storms at Oregon. Skiing will dwindle and floods will increase. Summers, however, will be drier than ever. The annual acreage burned by Oregon forest fires is expected to double by 2040, compared to 20th century levels.

The Earth's climate does change naturally in cycles. Our planet has seen other periods of warming. But the current rise in greenhouse gases is so far beyond anything in the geologic record that it's hard to forecast what will happen next.

What can we do? Should we switch our cars to alternative fuels like ethanol or hydrogen? Actually, although these alter-

By 2005 the Coe Glacier had lost much of its volume, cutting summer water supplies to irrigators in the Hood River Valley's orchards.

natives might reduce our dependence on foreign oil, studies show they don't really help with the overall emission of greenhouse gases. Smaller, lighter, more efficient vehicles are far more important. Bicycles are beautiful. Walking is wonderful.

Oregon is burdened with a special responsibility because our state is so heavily forested. Forests have been compared to the "lungs" of the planet. Trees absorb carbon dioxide during the day, lock up carbon, and pump out oxygen at night. Ancient forests are particularly efficient at this process, according to a study by OSU School of Forestry professor Beverly Law.

If we are to slow global warming, the effort must be global. China, for example, now puts more carbon dioxide into the atmosphere than the United States. But Americans still have a much greater impact per person.

Although we cannot change the world by ourselves, the changing climate is likely to transform us. The shrinking of glaciers over the past century is just one symptom of a deeper problem. Who can say how different Oregon's outdoors will look in another century?

30 CARL & TABLE LAKES

W ildfires have left a fringe of snags around the south and east sides of the Mt. Jefferson Wilderness. Hikers often look at the blackened trailheads and go elsewhere.

They're missing a bet. The most beautiful destinations are still green. Many are better than before because they're uncrowded. The trick is to hike through the burn.

The trail to Carl Lake is a prime example. If you're backpacking, this

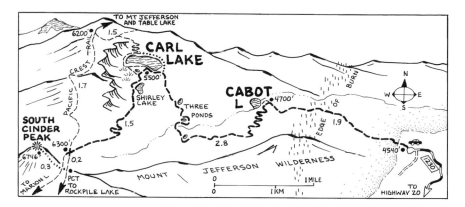

lake serves as the gateway to The Table, a rarely visited and completely unburned corner of the wilderness, on Mt. Jefferson's southeast shoulder.

Even on a day hike, there's lots to do at deep, rock-rimmed Carl Lake—explore the interesting shoreline, admire wildflowers, gather huckleberries, or take a challenging side trip to a viewpoint atop South Cinder Peak.

The trail starts in a 2003 fire zone.

The trail starts out through a recovering forest with snags, fireweed, chinkapin, and new views of Mt. Jefferson. After half a mile you'll start noticing trees that survived the 2003 blaze, and at the 1.6-mile mark you suddenly leave the burn behind. Notice, however, the wealth of blue huckleberries along the trail—a sign that this area too was thinned by fire long ago.

Carl Lake (below) makes a good day-hike goal.   Opposite: Mt. Jefferson from Table Lake.

At the 1.9-mile mark go briefly right on a short, unsigned side trail to inspect forest-rimmed Cabot Lake. Then return to the main path, which now heads uphill in earnest. After a dozen switchbacks the trail levels somewhat, passing a series of three scenic ponds. A final level stretch leads to large, blue-green Carl Lake.

The trail leads left around the south shore, past small heather meadows with purple aster and white partridge foot. Though there is no trail around the lake's north shore, the mountain views are better there, and the bared bedrock rim is quite hikable.

The north shore bears the marks of the Ice Age glacier that gouged out this lake's basin, polishing the bedrock smooth and sometimes grooving the surface as smaller rocks dragged beneath the heavy ice. Only a narrow rim now holds the lake back from the steep Cabot Creek Valley beyond. Atop this natural dam, bonsaied whitebark pines struggle in cracks. Clark's nutcrackers squawk, eyeing picnickers' sandwiches.

If you're backpacking, remember to camp more than 100 feet from the shore or trail.

Backpackers should consider making their second day's goal Table Lake. It's 5 miles north of Carl Lake, on a trail that dead-ends where the Warm Springs Indian Reservation slices into Mt. Jefferson's flank.

Don't be tempted by the romantically named "Hole-In-The-Wall Park" in this area. It's a viewless bog in a side canyon.

Table Lake, however, is a goal worth a journey. Springs amid wildflower meadows feed the lake. Mt. Jefferson rises like a snowy tower above the lake's forested rim. Because all of this is more than ten miles from the nearest trailhead, you might not

Mt. Jefferson, capped with a lenticular cloud, towers above The Table's heather.

see another person for days.

If that's not enough solitude, scramble up to The Table itself, between Table Lake and the Cascade crest. This mile-long alpine mesa has no trail access, but a rough route scales its southern rim. On top, a vast field of red heather stretches toward the biggest view of Mt. Jefferson ever.

Admittedly, the price of admission to this paradise is steep. But what a great hideaway!

Getting There: Turn off Highway 20 at the "Wilderness Trailheads" sign 8 miles east of Santiam Pass (or 12 miles west of Sisters), near milepost 88. Drive north 4.4 miles on paved Jack Lake Road 12 and turn left on one-lane Road 1230 for 1.6 miles of pavement and an additional 7 miles of gravel to road's end, following signs for the Cabot Lake Trailhead (GPS location N44 34.422' W121 43.890'.)

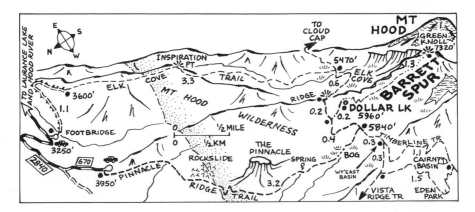

The Pinnacle Ridge Trail

A rguably the prettiest and quietest timberline meadows at Mt. Hood are on its north flank — on the opposite side of the mountain from the crowds at Timberline Lodge.

Hiking the Pinnacle Ridge Trail to these meadows is like stepping back to a time when all of the trails at Mt. Hood were small and rarely used.

If you're up for a short off-trail exploration on Barrett Spur you can make your goal Dollar Lake, a charming pond that's round as a coin.

The trail starts by climbing through mountain hemlock woods draped with witch's hair lichen. The forest is dark enough that the beargrass and huckleberry plants crowding the path rarely bloom. In the course of the

The Pinnacle Ridge Trail (at left) climbs the quiet north side of Mt. Hood, accessing Dollar Lake (above) and the wildflower meadows of Barrett Spur (below).

next 2 miles you'll cross a creek, skirt a rockslide, and get a distant glimpse of this ridge's namesake Pinnacle, a rock bluff in the woods. Then you climb through increasingly gorgeous meadows to the Timberline Trail.

Dollar Lake is less than a mile away, but it can be hard to find. The best plan is to hike left on the Timberline Trail 0.6 mile until it turns sharply to the right at a ridge end. Continue 100 feet to a breathtaking view of Elk Cove and Mt. Hood.

Then turn around and backtrack on the Timberline Trail 0.2 mile, watching closely for the unmarked, unofficial Dollar Lake trail. After 370 steps, when you reach a minor gully on the left with view of the tip of Mt. Hood, turn uphill on a little path that heads straight toward the mountain amid lupine, paintbrush, and Christmas-tree-sized hemlocks. In 0.2 mile you'll reach the 60-foot-wide lakelet.

Adventurers eager for grander views should look for a trail on the opposite side of Dollar Lake. This faint path switchbacks up onto Barrett Spur and follows its crest 1.3 miles amid lupine and krummholz (storm-bent alpine trees) to a green knoll at the head of Elk Cove's canyon.

This is as about as high as you should go on Mt. Hood without climbing equipment. At this point you're just a couple miles, by air, from the crowds of tourists at Timberline Lodge. But on lonely Barrett Spur, you'll feel like you're on a different mountain altogether.

A brook tumbles through heather meadows on Mt. Hood's Barrett Spur (at right).

Getting There: From Hood River, take Highway 35 south 13 miles, turn right near milepost 83 for 2 miles to a flashing light, and turn right for half a mile to Parkdale. Turn left beside the railroad station onto Clear Creek Road for 2.8 miles and fork to the right on Laurance Lake Drive for 4.2 paved, narrow miles to Kinnikinnick Campground at Laurance Lake. Then turn uphill to the left on gravel Road 2840 for 1.1 mile to a fork. To the left at this fork is the parking area for the Elk Cove Trail, a better-known rival of the Pinnacle Trail. But because a bridge washout has added more than a mile of climbing to the Elk Cove Trail, it's really not as nice. So fork to the right to stay on Road 2840 for another 1.8 miles. Then fork to the left on Road 670 for 0.7 mile to a parking area at road's end (GPS location N45 26.380' W121 41.408').

Hiking Tips: Walk back on the road 200 feet to find the trail. At the 2.3-mile mark you'll cross another small creek. Boots are good here because the tread vanishes into the steep, boggy meadow. Cross 100 feet to the far upper side of the field to find the trail where it reenters the woods. Then continue up through meadows 0.8 mile to a T-shaped junction with the Timberline Trail (GPS location N45 24.743' W121 42.557'). Turn left on the Timberline Trail 0.4 mile and turn uphill to the right on a faint, unmarked trail 0.2 mile to Dollar Lake (GPS location N45 24.675' W121 42.242'). If you're backpacking, don't camp in a meadow, nor near this fragile shore! Instead hide your tent on a wooded knoll to the left.

SCALING SOUTH SISTER

More people have been climbing South Sister recently, even though scientists have discovered that the mountain is bulging.

Of course the trip is popular for many reasons. The view at the summit covers half the state. The challenging trail to the top doesn't require technical climbing skill—just good weather and plenty of stamina.

But for some, the climb has become a chance to see Oregon's third tallest peak before it changes forever.

I recall turning down invitations to climb Mt. St. Helens before its 1980 eruption. Like most locals, I imagined the mountain's beautiful white cone would always be there. Since the 1980 blast, I've climbed to the edge of Mt. St. Helens' ragged, dusty crater. The climb is easier now that they've lowered the summit by 2000 feet, but it's not the same.

Volcanologists don't predict a similarly violent eruption for South Sister, at least not in the near future.

Before Mt. St. Helens blew up it was bulging at the rate of more than three feet a day. In the late 1990s South Sister was bulging about an inch a year. Since 2004 the pace has slowed to half an inch a year.

The ground deformation covers an 8-mile-wide zone centered 3 miles west of South Sister's summit. The change is so slight that scientists can measure it only with global positioning system satellites.

Still, the mountain's bulge is almost certainly caused by rising magma, a precursor to a possible eruption.

South Sister last erupted about 1200 years ago. Judging from the mountain's geologic record, the next eruption is likely to be a modest fireworks show, perhaps leaving a new cinder cone and lava flow.

Even a modest eruption, however, could change the wilderness scenery that visitors to South Sister take for granted, turning green alpine meadows gray.

If you'd like to see it before it's gone, here's what you need to know.

Climbing South Sister in a single day is a grueling, 11-mile trek, gaining 4900 feet of elevation.

If that sounds too demanding, consider turning back at Moraine Lake, halfway up the mountain. Not only is Moraine Lake less stark than the summit, but it also has better weather. The summit often generates its

The Green Lakes (at left) offer one possible climbing route to the summit of South Sister, but it's slightly shorter via Moraine Lake (below).

own wisp of clouds—a nuisance when you're at the top.

For the quickest route to the top, set out from Devils Lake on the South Sister Climbers Trail. This path crosses a footbridge over glassy Tyee Creek before crossing the highway. Then the trail launches steeply uphill through a dense mountain hemlock forest.

After 1.5 very steep, viewless miles, the path suddenly emerges from the forest at the edge of a vast, sandy plateau. South Sister and Broken Top loom ahead. Signs at a four-way trail junction indicate that Moraine Lake is to the right, but continue straight on the climbers' trail.

This portion of the hike is a lark—strolling up the open tableland, admiring views of a dozen mountains and lakes. Wind-gnarled trees pose in occasional clusters. Scraggly, red-leaved dogbane plants dot the sand.

Moraine Lake and Broken Top.

At the upper end of Moraine Lake's valley the trail swerves left around a rock outcrop. Just above this curve is a great lunch spot with a view. Boulders serve as tables and chairs.

Turn back here if you're planning to visit Moraine Lake. Hike back 1.1 mile to a fork in the trail and veer left down a sandy ridge to the lake. This ridge is the actual moraine—a pile of sand and rocks left by a glacier. The Lewis Glacier carved Moraine Lake's U-shaped valley in the Ice Age.

If you're intent on climbing South Sister, pause at the lunch stop viewpoint to assess the weather. If you can't see the summit, don't go on. What looks like a fluffy white cloud ahead can prove to be a dangerous blizzard at the top.

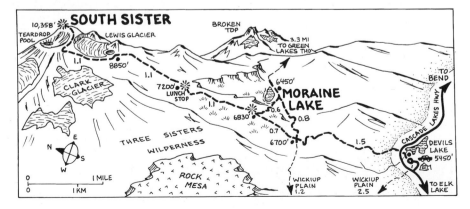

Above the lunch stop viewpoint, the trail steepens drastically, climbing 1.1 mile to a resting point in a sandy saddle—the current terminal moraine of the Lewis Glacier, overlooking a small green cirque lake.

After another 0.7 mile you'll crest the lip of South Sister's broad crater. Follow the rim to the right 0.4 mile to the summit, a rocky ridgecrest with a benchmark.

Bend, Sisters, and Redmond are clearly visible in the Central Oregon flatlands. To the north, the green Chambers Lakes dot the barren, glacial landscape below Middle Sister.

Teardrop Pool in the summit crater.

You might want to stretch your legs before your descent by ambling west across the broad summit crater to Teardrop Pool, a small blue lake locked in ice.

This is also the place to get a better look down the west side of the volcano, toward the region deformed by South Sister's bulge.

Many things could happen when South Sister next erupts. The mountain's glaciers could melt, launching mudflows and floods that race down the McKenzie River toward Eugene and Portland. Ash could turn the Three Sisters Wilderness gray. Cinders and lava could spark forest fires. The silhouette of the mountain could change.

Perhaps that uncertainty is one of the reasons to visit South Sister. To know what it was like before.

Getting There: Drive 28.5 miles west of Bend on the Cascade Lakes Highway. Beyond the Mt. Bachelor Ski Area 6.5 miles, turn left at a Devils Lake Trailhead sign and park at the end of the campground loop (GPS location N44 02.118' W121 45.953').

Tips for Visitors: Bring sunscreen and at least two quarts of water per person. Snow usually limits the climbing season to ten weeks, from about August 1 to mid October, but blizzards are possible even in August. Dogs are allowed only on leash, and because the cinders on South Sister cut paws, it's kindest to leave dogs at home. If you're planning to break up the climb by camping at Moraine Lake, note that tents within a quarter mile of the lake are allowed only at approved sites designated by a post. Space is tight on weekends, and campfires are banned.

PLAIKNI FALLS

A spring-fed waterfall cascades down the cliffy face of Anderson Bluffs at the end of this lovely, little-known trail in Crater Lake National Park. The one-mile packed gravel path is easy enough that it's accessible even to visitors in wheelchairs.

The path sets off across Kerr Valley, a remarkably flat-bottomed canyon carved by one of the glaciers that descended the flanks of Mt. Mazama in the Ice Age. Rivers tend to carve V-shaped valleys, but because glaciers are so heavy and broad they excavate U-shaped valleys instead. When Mt. Mazama erupted and collapsed to create Crater Lake about 7700 years ago, the valley was amputated, leaving Kerr Notch as a U-shaped dip in the caldera rim.

As Mt. Mazama collapsed, a glowing avalanche of superheated rock and ash raced down Kerr Valley, destroying all life for miles. Since then, Shasta red fir and mountain hemlock have managed to reforest the valley. Some of the trees are hundreds of years old and as much as two feet in diameter. Because of the deep winter snow and pumice soil at this elevation, there is virtually no underbrush.

Pink monkeyflowers (below) line the creek below Plaikni Falls, the goal of an easy one-mile trail that opened in 2011 at Crater Lake National Park.

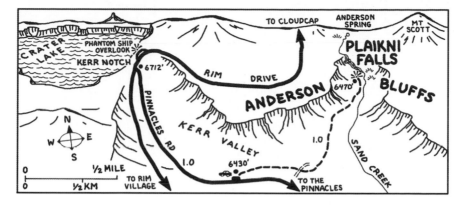

After 0.3 mile the trail crosses an abandoned roadbed, part of an old fire road to the park's eastern border. In the 1930s, this road was used to access a large quarry that extended to the left of the trail as far as Anderson Bluffs. Workers from the Civilian Conservation Corps (CCC) quarried rock from the cliffs to build viewpoint walkways and walls along Rim Drive. The forest is reclaiming the quarry site, although the trees there are still noticeably smaller.

The trail skirts the base of Anderson Bluffs and suddenly emerges from the woods at a meadow along Sand Creek. A few hundred feet later the trail ends at a rock-walled patio with a view of a 20-foot waterfall. Asked to choose a name for the cascade, the Klamath tribe picked *plaikni*, a Klamath word for waters from Crater Lake's high country.

Wildflowers crowding the brook here include blue lupine, pink monkeyflower, red paintbrush, and purple monkshood. To protect this fragile area, please don't leave the trail. Enjoy the wildflowers and the waterfall from the viewpoint, and then return as you came.

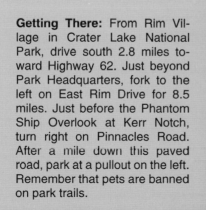

Getting There: From Rim Village in Crater Lake National Park, drive south 2.8 miles toward Highway 62. Just beyond Park Headquarters, fork to the left on East Rim Drive for 8.5 miles. Just before the Phantom Ship Overlook at Kerr Notch, turn right on Pinnacles Road. After a mile down this paved road, park at a pullout on the left. Remember that pets are banned on park trails.

Accessible to strollers and wheelchairs, the trail is part of a park effort to lure visitors away from the heavily used lake rim.

DIAMOND PEAK

When Eugene pioneer John Diamond was scouting an Oregon Trail shortcut across the Cascade Range in 1852, he climbed to the best viewpoint he could find and named it after himself.

The wagon route he blazed past 8744-foot Diamond Peak proved to be so sketchy that the 1027 pioneers who tried to follow the route the next year became known as the Lost Wagon Train.

Today it's still possible to become bewildered at Diamond's peak. There is no trail to the top. The top itself is a confusing collection of five different summits.

But not everyone who wanders here is lost. Even beginning hikers can follow a well-marked trail to Marie and Rockpile Lakes, a pair of lovely pools at the base of the mountain. No technical skills or rock-climbing gear are required to continue on to the summit—just lots of stamina and a knack for route-finding.

Set out on the Rockpile Trail, which climbs amid lodgepole pine, mountain hemlock, and subalpine fir. Blue huckleberries ripen along this lower part of the trail throughout August. The trees are festooned with the gray-green streamers of old man's beard lichen. Also known as usnea, this lichen is proof of the area's clean air. Because the lichen gathers all of its nutrients from the rain and the air, not from the trees, it quickly overdoses and dies in the presence of air pollution.

After 1.3 miles, go straight at an X-shaped junction. In the next mile the trail climbs alongside Diamond Rockpile, a rocky ridge where you won't find diamonds. It too was named for John Diamond. Nearby Pioneer Gulch and Emigrant Pass also honor the frontier route he scouted.

At the 2.1-mile mark the path crests at a viewpoint overlooking Summit Lake and a string of Cascade peaks (from left to right, Cowhorn Mountain, Sawtooth Mountain, and the spire of Mt. Thielsen). After another 0.4 mile, short trails lead left to Marie Lake and right to Rockpile Lake. These are both possible turnaround points. They have campable areas nearby, so you could make this your base for climbing Diamond Peak.

If you're headed for the summit, continue half a mile and turn left on the Pacific Crest Trail. The PCT offers glimpses ahead to Diamond Peak, but the first viewpoint south to Summit Lake and Mt. Thielsen comes after another 1.2 miles, when the PCT turns a sharp corner to the right on an open, rocky ridge. Note this trail "corner" well, because it is here that climbers face the decision of leaving trails behind.

If the weather is at all doubtful, or if someone in your group is not in top condition, or if you don't have a global positioning device to guarantee you can find this exact spot on the way down, don't attempt to climb Diamond Peak.

If you're headed for the top, however, walk 50 feet past the PCT's "corner." At a rock cairn, leave the trail and veer left up the rocky, open ridge. Cairns help guide you as far as timberline. Then simply continue straight up, crossing rockfields, loose sand, and some snow patches for a mile to what appears to be the mountain's summit.

For an easy hike at Diamond Peak, head for Marie Lake (below). Adventurers can continue to the summit, where the view extends across Waldo Lake to the Three Sisters (opposite).

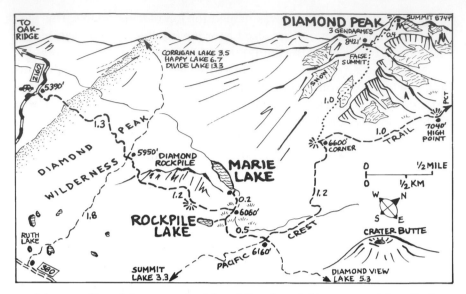

It's actually a false summit. Ahead lies the trickiest part of the climb—a rocky hogback. This awkward ridge includes three "gendarmes," rock spires blocking the crest. You have to use your hands, and a lot of caution, to work your way around these obstacles.

Then slog up a cinder pile to Diamond Peak's summit, where views unfold north across distant Waldo Lake to the Three Sisters, Mt. Jefferson, and the tip of Mt. Hood.

The hardest part of the climb is skirting rock gendarmes on a ridge to the summit.

Diamond Peak from a trailside meadow.

The biggest danger of the descent is missing the "corner" where you left the PCT. Mountain climbers rarely become disoriented on the way up because mountaintops are usually pretty obvious. When descending, however, angling a few degrees in the wrong direction can leave you miles from your car.

From the false summit, head straight toward Summit Lake and pointy Mt. Thielsen. If you end up in deep forest on a gentle slope, you've gone too far to the right (the west). This is when it's important to have a global positioning system device.

Since the Lost Wagon Train's difficulties here in 1853, Diamond Peak has suffered from a reputation as an easy place to become lost. But John Diamond was right to boast about the magnificent, map-like view from the top. And for those in the know, his peak remains the perfect spot for a quiet mountain getaway.

Getting There: To find the Rockpile Trailhead from Eugene, drive Willamette Highway 58 east to Oakridge, continue 1.8 miles beyond town, and turn right at a "Hills Creek Dam" sign between mileposts 37 and 38. After half a mile bear right onto Road 21 and follow this paved route 29.2 miles. Beyond Indigo Springs Campground 0.4 mile, turn left on gravel Pioneer Gulch Road 2149 for 3.5 miles, and then turn right on Rockpile Road 2160 for 2.3 miles. Ignore the Pioneer Gulch Trailhead and continue to a sign on the left marking the Rockpile Trail (GPS location N43 29.014' W122 10.609'). Park on the road's wide, right-hand shoulder 200 feet beyond.

Hiking Tips: Mosquitoes bedevil this area in late July and early August, so it's best to wait until at least mid-August. From the trailhead, hike 2.5 miles to a T-shaped trail junction. The trail to the left deadends in 0.2 mile at Marie Lake (GPS location N43 29.628' W122 08.715'). To find Rockpile Lake, take the trail to the right 200 yards to a rock cairn, and detour 200 yards on a spur to the right.

Climbing Tips: To continue up Diamond Peak, return 200 yards from Rockpile Lake and turn right on the main trail half a mile to an X-shaped junction. Turn left on the Pacific Crest Trail for 1.2 miles until the PCT turns a corner to the right on an open, rocky ridge (GPS location N43 30.272' W122 08.542'). At a rock cairn 50 feet beyond this trail "corner", leave the trail and scramble straight up a ridge to the left for a mile to a false summit. Then continue on a narrow, dangerous ridge 0.4 mile to the actual summit.

LOVE OF LAVA: THE BLACK WILDERNESS

Where in Oregon can you camp at a lake that no human has visited before?

I believe this is possible in the Mt. Washington Wilderness, less than 4 miles from the paved McKenzie Pass Highway. To test this theory, I led an off-trail backpacking trek around Mt. Washington.

We learned why no one had probably been there before.

Known as the "Black Wilderness" for its miles of jagged lava flows, the rock landscape north of McKenzie Pass is so hostile that it's difficult to scramble even a few hundred yards without a trail.

An easier way to sample this landscape is to hike the Pacific Crest Trail to Little Belknap Crater, where crews with dynamite have blasted a path across the barrens.

Much of the raw-looking lava here comes from Belknap Crater and its dark twin, Little Belknap. Both mountains keep a low profile among the High Cascades' peaks, yet on average they've erupted every 1000 years since the Ice Age.

About 3000 years ago, eruptions in this area spilled so much lava to the west that two different flows blocked the McKenzie River. The upper flow dammed Clear Lake, drowning a forest that is still visible as underwater snags in the lake's crystal water.

A separate lava flow buried four miles of the McKenzie River between Koosah Falls and Tamolitch Dry Falls. Instead of pooling up permanently, the river found its way underground through lava tube caves. To this day the McKenzie flows underground on this stretch, emerging as underwater springs in Tamolitch Pool at the base of a dry "waterfall" (see page 66).

About 30 square miles of lava remain from these eruptions. Only a few tortured trees have managed to colonize the rock. But there are "islands" in the lava, where the flows parted around hills or cinder cones. Lakes have formed on many of these lava islands, isolated for millennia.

To explore the area, I planned a 19-mile trip through the lava fields one summer. We would start at Hand Lake, circle Mt. Washington off trail, and return on the Pacific Crest Trail to McKenzie Pass.

It proved to be the most dangerous hiking adventure I have ever led.

Nine experienced backpackers from the Obsidian outdoor club of Eugene and the Chemeketan club of Salem signed up. I required each of them to bring a full gallon of water, sturdy boots, and a large hat.

We met at the Hand Lake Trailhead on the McKenzie Pass Highway, strolled 2 miles north on a good trail, and then struck off along the sandy edge of a lava flow. It was a warm day, so when we reached a largish lake, we went for a swim. Then our route took us north across half a mile of lava.

By then the temperature had soared into the 90s. Balancing our heavy backpacks as we clambered up and down over the lava outcrops, the crossing took two hours. More than one person fell, tried to catch himself with an outstretched hand, and cut a palm to ribbons on the lava.

We drank up our gallons of water.

When we finally reached a lava island with a lake, we dumped our packs, stripped, and floated in the water for an hour.

Only when we were setting up

Few trails cross the lava beds at McKenzie Pass. Above, backpackers bushwhack along the edge of a flow with a view of Mt. Washington. Opposite: North and Middle Sister.

our tents did we realize that there were no cleared tent sites at this lava-bound lake. There were no campfire rings and no litter. In fact there was no trace of prior human presence at all. The only footprints in the dust were from birds, deer, and coyotes.

We slept that night as silent and lonely as colonists on a distant planet.

The next day was hotter still, and we had two full miles of lava to cross. Heat shimmered from the rock. Sweat dripped from the handkerchiefs we tied about our foreheads.

Although we had all refilled our water bottles from the lake so that we could carry a gallon apiece, some of us held back on drinking. By noon we were still in the lava. Those who had drained their water supplies were teetering, dangerously red-faced.

We rested under the sparse shade of a scraggly tree, assessing our

situation. We had gone too far to turn back.

We redistributed the few drops we had left to mop our brows and wet our tongues. Then we staggered on in the afternoon heat.

Night was falling by the time we collapsed on a forested ridge of Mt. Washington. We sent three of

the strongest hikers ahead to fetch water from a boggy pond at timberline.

I think none of us remembers dinner that evening. All that mattered was water and sleep.

The third day of that difficult trek took us over two ridges on the east-

ern flank of Mt. Washington. We swam in trailless George Lake, found the Pacific Crest Trail with delight, and followed this wilderness freeway toward McKenzie Pass.

By then the heat had conjured up a lightning storm. Bolts crashed into the hills on either hand. A forest fire sprang to life two miles away near the Matthieu Lakes. Smoke drifted across the pass. Helicopters shuttled water buckets overhead.

No one died on my backpack through the Black Wilderness, but I did have trouble recruiting people for a trip the next year.

This is why I'm recommending that you sample the lava with a hike to Little Belknap Crater on the relatively safe Pacific Crest Trail.

This hike follows the lava flow to its source in a throat-shaped

Lava flows near Mt. Washington (above) include many forested "islands", some of them with rarely visited lakes (at left).

147

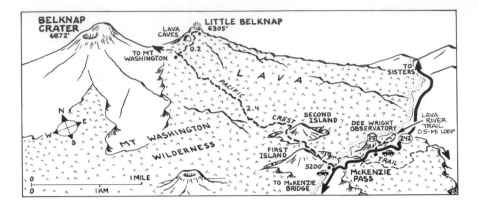

cave atop Little Belknap. Along the way you'll pass lava bombs, pressure ridges, and forested islands left in the aftermath of the eruption. Tennis shoes aren't recommended on the path's jagged lava cinders.

When you park at the Pacific Crest Trailhead near McKenzie Pass, the start of the trail's tread is not clear in the sand and dust of this sparse pine forest. Walk to the message board and head left past the "Mt. Washington Wilderness" sign. Climb 0.4 mile along the edge of an "island" surrounded by lava, then cross the blocky flow for 100 yards to the second "island"—another hill that succeeded in diverting the liquid basalt.

Notice how the sunny south slope of the hill has dry manzanita and ponderosa pine, while the cooler north slope is damp enough to support huckleberry and subalpine fir.

At the 0.8-mile mark the trail climbs onto the lava for good. Why is the flow so rugged? After the surface solidified, liquid basalt flowed on underneath the crust, buckling up pressure ridges and leaving caves that often collapsed. Since then, only a few intrepid whitebark pines and penstemons have managed to take root.

Getting There: Drive McKenzie Highway 242, the scenic old road between Sisters and McKenzie Bridge. Half a mile west of McKenzie Pass, at a small hiker-symbol sign near milepost 77, turn north into a parking area (GPS locataion N44 15.604' W121 48.587'). The Pacific Crest Trail heads north across the lava toward Little Belknap Crater.

Views improve of North and Middle Sister as you climb. Ahead is Belknap Crater's red cone, whose eruption blanketed 100 square miles with ash. Blobs of molten rock were thrown high into the air and solidified in teardrop shapes—the lava "bombs" along the slope.

Near the trail's crest, a rock cairn with a pole marks the junction to Little Belknap. Turn right

OREGON FAVORITES

on a 0.2-mile path to the summit parapet. The last 50 feet are a steep scramble to a viewpoint of peaks from Mt. Jefferson to Broken Top.

On the way back down to the trail junction, stop to explore the lava caves. Actually, these are three short remnants of a single collapsed tube. Since the caves offer the only shade on this hike, they make tempting lunch spots. The uppermost cave, 50 feet north of the path, has a 40-foot-deep throat with snow at the bottom. Don't fall in! Farther down the trail, walk through the middle cave's culvert-like tube. The lowest cave, just south of the trail, is a low-ceilinged bunker.

If you'd like a slightly better view, you can scramble up Belknap Crater. Continue north on the PCT until it leaves the lava. Then head cross-country, traversing left to the cinder cone's less-steep northern slope.

And of course, if you're prepared, you're welcome to strike out cross-country through the lava.

Only in the "Black Wilderness" are you likely to find a secret lake that you can truly call your own.

The spire of Mt. Washington rises above the PCT on its route to Little Belknap.

SEPTEMBER
IN OREGON

*Middle and North Sister from Tam
Lake, below Tam McArthur Rim*

RIM WITH A VIEW
AT BROKEN TOP

S urrounded by sheer, 500-foot cliffs, Tam McArthur Rim has an almost aerial view of the Three Sisters.

This rim is one of my favorite August getaways, and not just
because of the view. The trail here deadends in the relatively uncrowded heart of the Three Sisters Wilderness—Oregon's most popular backwoods retreat.

If you are willing to continue beyond trail's end, you can roam through

The trail atop Tam McArthur Rim's 500-foot cliff climbs toward Broken Top.

spectacular, Sound-of-Music alpine scenery to three hidden lakes where crowds are unknown.

Even in August a few patches of snow remain among the struggling trees and wildflowers of the rim's tablelands. Although hiking to the brink of this enormous fault scarp is not difficult, you arrive at an elevation greater than that of many Oregon mountains.

The rim's name honors Lewis ("Tam") A. McArthur, secretary of the Oregon Geographic Names Board from 1916 to 1949.

The path starts out with a steady climb for 0.7 mile to reach the rim's plateau. Then you climb more gradually for half a mile across the rim's tilted tableland before views begin to unfold. To the north, look for (left to right) Belknap Crater, Mt. Washington, Three Fingered Jack, Mt. Jefferson, Mt. Hood, and the tip of Mt. Adams.

The wildflowers of this sandy plateau grow in scattered clumps to preserve moisture and to fight the winds. The bright purple trumpets are penstemon. The clumps of yellow balls are sulfur plant. And the off-white, fuzzy flowers are dirty socks—source of a suspicious odor wafting across the hot sand.

OREGON FAVORITES

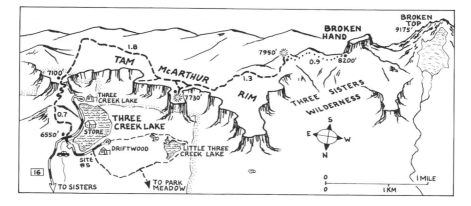

Finally, at an unmarked fork, take a small right-hand path 200 yards along the rim to the cliff-edge viewpoint. Three Creek Lake and its cousin, Little Three Creek Lake, are over 1000 feet below. To the east, sunlight glints off metal roofs in Bend and Sisters. To the south is snowy Mt. Bachelor, striped with ski slopes.

The cliff-edge viewpoint is a perfectly good turnaround point, but it's worth exploring farther toward Broken Top on a relatively level 1.3-mile continuation of the trail. Return to the main trail and turn right toward Broken Top.

After a mile of sandy, alpine country, climb a snowfield and turn left up what appears to be a small red cinder cone—but which is in fact a ridge end. Stop at the ridgecrest amid a scattering of drop-shaped lava bombs, and admire the view here stretching south to Mt. Thielsen.

This is where the off-trail adventures to the hidden lakes begin. Map, compass, and route-finding skills are essential. Attempt these treks only if the weather is excellent.

The most astonishing day-hike goal is an iceberg-dotted moraine lake in Broken Top's crater, 1.5 miles farther to the west on the ridge. To get there, continue along the ridge on an unofficial trail that contours on the steep left side of a spire called Broken Hand. The path is faint and very rough, but it doesn't gain much elevation.

Don't expect to see the crater lake until the last minute, when

Getting There: Drive Highway 20 to downtown Sisters and turn south on Elm Street at a sign for Three Creek Lake. Follow Elm Street and its successor, Road 16, for 15.7 miles. After 1.7 miles of gravel (and a mile beyond the Three Creek Meadow horse camp), notice the trailhead sign on the left, opposite the entrance road to Driftwood Campground. Park at a lot 100 feet down the campground road and walk back to the trail.

you explore through a V-shaped notch in the sandy moraine at the base of Broken Top's crags. No trees grow in this windy alpine barrens, and there is no level ground, so it's not a place for backpackers.

Adventurers looking for a campsite should head for a pair of trailless pools in the woods—Tam Lake and Rim Lake. Both have terrific views of the mountains, but because they are nearly 2 miles from any official trail, they're pretty quiet.

From the end of the official trail at Tam McArthur Rim (1.3 miles beyond the cliff-edge viewpoint), cross the snowfield to the base of what appears to be a small, red cinder cone, but instead of climbing the cinder slope, veer right to a pass.

The edge of the rim here is not a cliff, but rather a rocky slope crossed by animal trails. Pick your way down the far side and contour due northwest for 2 miles. Then look for an unofficial horse trail that leads up to the right to Tam Lake. Slightly larger Rim Lake is just beyond.

If you're backpacking, remember that campsites should be at least 100 feet from any water source, so don't camp on a fragile lakeshore.

My wife and I once tented here on the busiest weekend of summer and had the place to ourselves. We returned to our car on a loop by bushwhacking down Tam Lake's outlet creek 1.8 miles to the Park Meadow Trail—a wide path that's hard to miss. Then we turned right for 3.7 miles; just before Road 16 a trail to the right leads 2 miles to Three Creeks Lake and the parking area for the Tam McArthur Rim Trail.

The trailless alpine meadows around Broken Top are full of secret places. Don't tell.

Lava bombs (above) litter the alpine landscape near the icy lake in Broken Top's crater (at left).

37

TIMBERLINE LODGE

Mt. Hood's Timberline Lodge began as a Depression-era make-work program, but by the time President Roosevelt dedicated this elegantly rustic hotel in 1937 it had become a grand expression of Northwest art. Surprisingly few visitors to the lodge venture into the scenic alpine landscape that lured hotel builders here in the first place. Three top goals await hikers: the Silcox Hut, Zigzag Canyon, and Paradise Park.

The Silcox Hut served as the upper terminus for Timberline's original Magic Mile ski lift from 1939 to 1962. Reopened as a chalet in 1992, it now offers overnight bunks for groups and a limited cafe in the European alpine tradition. To hike there, walk past the right-hand side of Timberline Lodge and follow a paved walkway uphill 200 yards. Turn right on the Pacific Crest Trail across a snow gully for 100 feet and then turn uphill

Starting at Timberline Lodge (above), the Timberline Trail soon leaves crowds behind as it sets out clockwise around Mt. Hood (below).

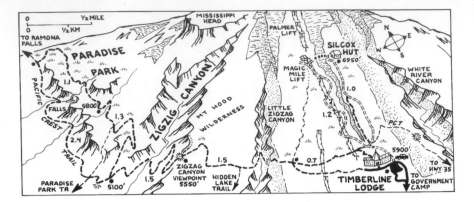

onto the Mountaineer Trail, a braided path through wind-gnarled firs and August-blooming blue lupine. After 0.6 mile, join a dirt road for the remainder of the climb to the hut.

For a more wilderness-oriented hike, take the Pacific Crest Trail to Zigzag Canyon or Paradise Park. Start by walking past the right-hand side of Timberline Lodge on a wide, paved walkway uphill. After 200 yards turn left on the Pacific Crest Trail amidst lupine and cushion-shaped clumps of white phlox. This path ducks under a chairlift and contours through gorgeous wildflower meadows with views south to Mt. Jefferson and the Three Sisters. At the 1-mile mark the path dips into a 200-foot-deep gully to cross the Little Zigzag River on stepping stones (a possible turnaround point for hikers with small children). Continue another easy 1.2 miles to an overlook of Zigzag Canyon, a 700-foot-deep chasm gouged into Mt. Hood's cindery flank by the glacier-fed Zigzag River.

Keep left at this point, continuing 1.5 miles on the PCT, which switchbacks down through the forest to cross the huge gorge. The Zigzag River is usually small enough here that you can hop across on rocks. At a trail junction on the far side of the canyon, turn right onto the Paradise Loop Trail and climb another mile to meadows stuffed with August wildflowers: fuzzy cats ears, red paintbrush, blue lupine, and white bistort—a rank little fuzzball also known as "dirty socks."

To complete the loop, keep straight on the Paradise Loop Trail until it crosses a big creek and reaches a bare area—the site of a stone shelter smashed by a falling tree in 1994 and painstakingly removed. From the shelter site, head slightly uphill (north) to find a path traversing left below a cliffy bluff. This path leads 1.1 mile through heather fields before descending to the PCT. Then turn left for 2.4 miles to return to Zigzag Canyon and the route back.

Blue lupine fills a swale in Paradise Park, on the Timberline Trail west of the lodge.

Getting There: From Portland, drive Highway 26 toward Mt. Hood 54 miles. On the far side of Government Camp, turn left for 6 miles up to Timberline Lodge's parking lot.

38

Every September, Oregon grocery stores showcase fresh local chan-terelles—the peppery orange mushrooms that cook up in butter with a flavorful firmness that makes gourmets swoon.

Of course, collecting wild mushrooms is never safe for the uninitiated. But chanterelles are relatively hard to confuse with poisonous toadstools. And the edible ribbed mushrooms sprout in droves along Oregon's coast-al forest trails for free.

A prime place for chanterelle hunting is along the 6.4-mile loop hike to Tahkenitch Lake. Even if you don't give fungus a second glance, the trip makes a great outing. The loop visits giant sand dunes, a three-mile-long lake, and a lonely stretch of beach.

The path starts out climbing past 20-foot-tall rhododendrons that bloom in April and May. Keep left at a junction after 0.2 mile.

The trail traverses through woods, cutting across the toe of an advanc-ing sand dune and zigzagging around a ridge. This is where you'll find chanterelles, often budding from the disturbed soil where the tread cuts into the duff.

Unlike the many native plants that prefer old-growth woods, chanterelles like disturbed soil in young forests.

ENCHANTED AT TAHKENITCH DUNES

Threemile Lake really is 3 miles long, bordered by the coastal Tahkenitch Dunes.

Bring a guidebook or an expert to help you identify chanterelles. Look under the cap to make sure the mushroom does not have white papery gills, but rather has ribbed orange ridges that run down onto the stalk. Edible chanterelles grow out of the forest duff, and never out of dead logs or stumps.

Do not pull up chanterelles. Cut them off with a knife so the fungus in the ground survives to sprout another day.

Always rely on a guide when gathering wild mushrooms. Chanterelles have ribs that run down their stalks (below left). Never touch poisonous panther amanitas (below right). Unlike chanterelles, amanitas have papery white gills unconnected to their stalks.

At the 2.9-mile mark the trail crosses a bridge at the head of Threemile Lake. Then the path climbs to a campsite on a sandy bluff overlooking the lake.

Threemile Lake is in fact 3 miles long, but it's wedged between such steep slopes that the best access to the lakeshore is a 200-foot sand slide straight down from this viewpoint.

Scientists have unearthed saltwater mussel shells from prehistoric campsites along the lake, a find suggesting that this was once a salty estuary connected to the sea.

For the loop, follow signs across the dunes 0.4 mile to the ocean beach (GPS location N43° 47.33' W124° 10.36)'. Then turn right for a mile along

Huckleberries (above) and mushrooms grow along the Tahkenitch Dunes trail in fall. Below, the beach near Tahkenitch Creek is closed to motor vehicles to protect birds.

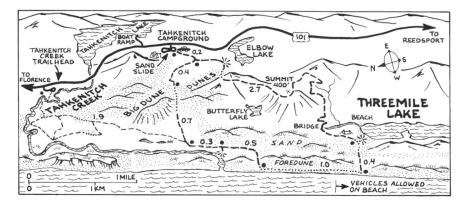

the surf. After 0.3 mile you'll pass a large steel I-beam planted in the sand with a sign announcing the end of an area where vehicles are permitted. You shouldn't see any tire tracks beyond this.

After a mile along the beach, head inland at a small sign (GPS location N43° 46.57' W124° 10.57'). The trail heads through overgrown sand dunes half a mile to a junction at the mouth of the Tahkenitch Creek estuary.

Then keep right for a mile, following posts across the Tahkenitch Dunes.

Exploring the sand hills here is like playing in a giant sandbox.

On the far side of the dunes, a signpost marks the trail into the woods. Then keep left for 0.6 mile to return to the Tahkenitch Campground trailhead.

Getting There: Drive Highway 101 south of Florence 13 miles (or north of Reedsport 8 miles). Between mileposts 203 and 204, turn west into Tahkenitch Campground, and then go straight into a trailhead parking loop. Parking passes are required, but can be bought here.

THE RIDDLES OF STEENS MOUNTAIN

Riddle me this: How many bachelor cowboys does it take to create a historic ranch district in a scenic desert canyon?

The answer is three, if we're talking about the Riddle Brothers Ranch National Historic District in the midst of southeast Oregon's Steens Mountain Wilderness.

Three brothers—Fred, Ben, and Walt Riddle—built pioneer plank-and-log ranchhouses along the Little Blitzen River in the early 1900s. The three Riddles died childless, and the Bureau of Land Management later bought the area for preservation.

Fred Riddle's ranch house (below) has been preserved in the Steens Mountain canyons, where sunsets cast long shadows (above).

The restored ranches recall a simpler, Old West lifestyle, with kerosene lamps, woodstoves, and barns full of horse gear. The ranch complex and the nearby South Steens Campground also serve as starting points for hikers exploring trails along the Little Blitzen River. An easy 1.5-mile path downstream from Fred Riddle's cabin is popular with fly fisher-

men and hikers with children. A longer route up Little Blitzen Gorge prowls the rugged high country of Steens Mountain.

The Riddle brothers were the third generation of a pioneer Oregon family that founded the town of Riddle south of Roseburg.

The family's Oregon adventures began in 1850 when William and Maximilla Riddle were farming in Illinois. That fall a neighbor, Isaac Constant, returned from a trek to Oregon with a vial of California gold dust and wondrous stories about the farmland that could be homesteaded for free in Oregon.

William and Maximilla promptly sold their 200-acre farm for $3000, packed up their eight children (aged two to adult), and headed west in early April, 1851 with three wagons, a carriage, and 40 head of cattle. They chose the less popular Applegate Trail through northern Nevada. Although the route was rugged, their entire entourage arrived intact in the Cow Creek Valley near present-day Riddle in late September.

A generation later, most of the Riddle family was still in Riddle,

A footbridge (above left) accesses the Fred Riddle ranch, with its tool shed (above right) and farm machinery (below left).

with the exception of Tobias Stilley Riddle. Stilley, as he was called, married Sarah Smyth and moved with her family in 1872 to homestead the Harney County grasslands near present-day Burns. Sarah's father and brother were killed by Indians in the Bannock War of 1878, but Stilley and Sarah Riddle stayed on.

Then Pete French arrived in Harney County. An ambitious cattle baron with wealthy

The head of Little Blitzen Canyon.

California connections, French bought out the Riddles for $30,000 in gold. Suddenly wealthy, Stilley and Sarah rejoined the rest of the Riddle clan in Western Oregon.

The Riddle family's involvement in Eastern Oregon might have ended there, but the three young sons of Stilley and Sarah had come to love the pungent smell of sage in the high desert. And so Fred, Ben, and Walt Riddle returned to take up homestead ranches on Steens Mountain between 1896 and 1909.

The three Riddle bachelors raised mules, herded them south to the rail line at Winnemucca, and sold them to the US Army cavalry. They raised cattle and irrigated hayfields. They brewed moonshine from a still, read

Getting There: From Bend, take Highway 20 east 134 miles to Burns. Fill your gas tank here. Then continue east on Highway 78 toward Crane for 1.7 miles, and turn right on paved Highway 205 for 61 miles to Frenchglen. For reservations at the Frenchglen Hotel, call 541-493-2825. To continue to the Riddle Ranch, drive past Frenchglen on the paved highway towards Fields for another 10 miles and then turn left onto the gravel Steens Mountain Loop Road for 19.5 miles. (This route is gated closed from about Thanksgiving to late May each year.) Stop at the well-marked South Steens Campground. The first campground entrance is for equestrians. The second entrance has family campsites amidst junipers and sagebrush. Cold drinking water is available from a spigot on a well house.

To find the Riddle Ranch, drive back from the campground on the Steens Mountain Loop Road 0.3 mile toward Frenchglen. At a sign for the ranch, turn right (north) on a dirt road for 1.3 miles to a parking area by a gate. The road ahead is closed to vehicles from October to mid-June, but even when the road is open in summer it's simply too rough for passenger cars. So unless you have a high-clearance rig, park at the gate and walk 1.3 miles to road's end at the Fred Riddle ranch.

books, played records on a Victrola, and complained about who had to do the cooking. Fred kept ten cats, feeding them three gallons of milk every morning and evening.

By 1952, when only Fred remained, he sold the entire ranch complex to Rex Clemens, a Philomath lumberman who had decided to get into the ranching business. After Rex Clemens died, his widow Ethel sold the ranchland to the BLM with the provision that the family cattle operation be allowed to continue.

A bachelor cowboy's kitchen.

Today a ranch cowboy and a small cattle herd remain, adding authenticity to what might otherwise be just another Old West museum. Cattle are not allowed on the vast Steens Mountain Wilderness that surrounds the 1120-acre ranch.

The drive to the Riddle Ranch takes you through the village of Frenchglen, where you can see another side of the area's pioneer heritage. Named for Pete French and his financial partner James Glenn, the tiny hamlet of Frenchglen features a 1916 hotel that has been restored by the Oregon State Parks.

The Frenchglen Hotel still has no public telephone or television. Rooms rent for less than $100 for a double bed, even if you choose the new wing out back with private baths. For meals, guests pack family-style around two large tables in the hotel lobby. Typical fare is herb-baked chicken with garlic roast potatoes and marionberry pie.

If you'd rather camp closer to the Riddle Ranch, drive another 30 miles to the South Steens Campground. Whether or not you stay here, this is a good landmark for finding the Riddle Ranch. The ranch is only 3 miles away, but the road there is so bad that you'll probably end up walking the last bit.

At road's end you cross a footbridge over the rushing, 15-foot-wide Little Blitzen River. On the far side is Fred Riddle's ranch house, with a big enclosed porch and a drafty second floor. Walk around the house to visit a cook's bunkhouse, a root cellar, a tool shed, a corral, and a barn.

Throughout the summer months, volunteer caretakers are on hand to answer questions.

For an easy hike along the river, recross the footbridge to the end of the road and go up a steep little trail near an outhouse. This path becomes an ancient roadbed that meanders downriver in a canyon lined with rimrock.

After 0.2 mile you'll pass a pioneer corral made of woven branches. Another 0.4 mile downstream the route forks, with the roadbed climbing left while a rough trail descends to the right along the river. Either route works, because they rejoin.

Continue another 0.9 mile to trail's end at a meadow where the Little Blitzen River joins the larger Donner und Blitzen River.

This is a lovely spot to lie in the grass and watch the glassy rivers merge. Butterflies flit past. Trout dart in the water. It's easy to see why the Riddle brothers liked the place.

For a longer hike to a giant gorge at the headwaters of the Little Blitzen River, try a different trail nearby. Drive back to the South Steens Campground entrance and continue east on the Steens Mountain Loop Road.

This upper part of the loop road is gated closed to vehicles from November through June. Even if the gate's closed, you can walk up the road half a mile to the Little Blitzen Trailhead parking area on the right. The trail itself starts 100 yards farther up the road on the left-hand side.

This trail up the Little Blitzen River enters a spectacular canyon lined with 1000-foot cliffs. The gorge traces the curving route of a long-vanished Ice Age glacier ten miles to its abrupt end at a semicircular headwall cliff just below the summit of Steens Mountain.

The trail up Little Blitzen Gorge quickly becomes a faint, braided path among wildflowers, sagebrush, and quaking aspen.

Deep in the Steens Mountain Wilderness, this is a route for adventurers—a place lost in time, true to the spirit of the pioneering Riddles.

Some scrambling is required to climb the headwall of Little Blitzen River's gorge.

HUCKLEBERRYING AT DIVIDE LAKE

The trail to Divide Lake is not only one of state's prettiest autumn hikes, but it's also one of the likelier places to hunt huckleberries.

Divide Lake fills a miniature cove with views south to broad Diamond Peak and north to craggy Mt. Yoran. Open, alpine terrain like this is rare in the Diamond Peak Wilderness, where dense mountain hemlock forests block most views.

Red huckleberry bushes grow low to the ground in the high country here. The red berries are perfectly edible, but were usually avoided by native tribes because of taboos.

Even today, people rarely bother to pick the red berries because they're so small and sparse. In the fall the bushes are attractive primarily because their leaves turn scarlet, firing the alpine meadows with color.

Two varieties of edible blue huckleberries—shiny blue and dull blue—grow at lower elevations in the Diamond Peak Wilderness. Both are more likely to fill your collecting cup with enough fruit for a pie. No promises! Some years the bushes just don't produce.

The trail starts in a young forest with a view ahead to Diamond Peak's

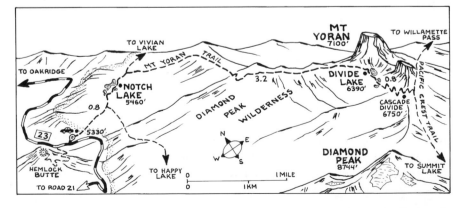

OREGON FAVORITES

snowy ridges and Mt. Yor-
an's massive plug. Then
the path enters old-growth
mountain hemlock woods
with blue huckleberry
bushes. After 0.6 mile ignore the Diamond Peak
Tie Trail branching off to
the right. This connector
allows backpackers to trek
around Diamond Peak in a
giant loop.

A few hundred yards
beyond the Tie Trail junction you'll reach Notch
Lake. Continue to the
lake's far end for the best
overview of this scenic,
rock-rimmed pool. On a
hot day, this lake warms
up enough to make for nice
swimming.

At a trail junction 0.2
mile beyond Notch Lake,
turn right onto the Mt. Yoran Trail. This path climbs
in earnest for 1.6 miles
before leveling off along a
ridgecrest. The ridge has
occasional views south to
Diamond Peak and north
across Salt Creek's forested
valley.

*Divide Lake fills a high basin between Diamond Peak
and Mt. Yoran (above).*

After a mile along the ridge, Mt. Yoran's massive monolith suddenly
appears above the woods ahead. Then the trail contours to the right across
a rockslide to Divide Lake.

Though very small, this blue-green lake is fortuitously situated to reflect different peaks from different shores. Walk around the shore to the
right, following a pointer labeled "Pacific Crest Trail." Notice how the
rock at the far end of the lake has been rounded and polished by the Ice
Age glacier that carved this scenic basin.

A bit farther along the trail you'll find a second heather-rimmed lake. If you're backpacking, be a sport and pitch camp out of sight of these delicate lakelets so other visitors won't find tents in their scenery.

Few hikers to Divide Lake will be able to resist continuing 0.8 mile up the trail to the actual divide—a pass with a view down the forested eastern slope of the Diamond Peak Wilderness.

If you still have lots of energy when you hike back to your car, or if you haven't yet found enough huckleberries, consider a short side trip up Hemlock Butte. From the Divide Lake trailhead, drive 200 yards back on Road 23 to a hiker-symbol sign at the pass. A steepish half-mile trail here gains 500 feet of elevation to a former lookout tower site atop a rocky knob with a panoramic view.

Seen from the trail to Divide Lake, Diamond Peak is a broad mountain with many peaks.

Memories at Jefferson Park

For decades my father would take a "last hike of summer" to Jefferson Park each September. Whenever I visit this alpine Shangri-La in the Mt. Jefferson Wilderness, where lake-dotted meadows snug against Oregon's second tallest mountain, I think of Dad.

Wes Sullivan had learned that the best-kept secret of the High Cascades is Indian summer, after the crowds of hikers and mosquitoes are gone. This is particularly true in Jeff Park. In autumn, huckleberry bushes

spread a four-inch-tall carpet of blue fruit and flaming red leaves across the lakeside meadows. Mt. Jefferson rises from the plain like a wall, its top often dusted with a skiff of new snow.

When I was young my Dad worked long hours as news editor of Salem's *Oregon Statesman*. He stayed up until 2am to put the paper to bed. The stress of deadlines led many of his colleagues to smoke, drink, and die young. Not Dad. He went hiking. Eventually the editor gave him a camera to take along. On slow news days, a surprising number of mountain photos wound up on the front page of Salem's paper.

When Dad became editor himself he wrote a weekly column, sometimes about his adventures hiking with my mother Elsie. One headline, "50 Miles at 50", celebrated their trek from McKenzie Pass to Jefferson Park on the year of their fiftieth birthdays. A decade later they hiked 60 miles for their 60th birthdays. Dad suggested they might defeat age indefinitely in this manner.

One of his columns recounted the September my parents took an electronic mosquito repeller to Jefferson Park. Dad wrote:

> The latest and most status-producing item in the competitive field of outdoor gear is a small, battery-operated box that emits a high-pitched sound. Its makers in Dallas, Texas, declare the sound is abhorrent to female mosquitoes. They are the ones that bite.
>
> My wife and I took the device up 6000 feet to Jefferson Park in search of the wily mosquito. It was a unique experience, hunting for mosquitoes instead of trying to avoid them. The weekend was a glorious success in terms of the beauty of the park and the late wildflowers, but a dismal failure as a mosquito hunt. We sighted only

In September, the huckleberry plants not only have fruit, but also scarlet leaves.

OREGON FAVORITES

two. My wife swatted one in a reflex action before I could bring the repeller to bear on it.

The other insect just sat there happily next to the buzzing repeller while my wife and I argued whether it was indeed a mosquito and whether it was male or female.

A later conversation with the owner of the outdoor store where we had purchased the electronic device drew the comment that "Some people swear by them and others swear at them."

But in terms of outdoors status, the actual field effectiveness of the repellent is of secondary consideration. Until the fickle fancy of mosquito fighters moves on to a more esoteric means of disposing of the pesky bugs, we have the most prestigious repellent of them all. We are "in."

Alzheimer's disease stole my mother from us, bit by bit, in the three years after her 70th birthday.

The September after she passed away Dad invited every male in the family to join him on his annual visit to Jeff Park.

A framed picture from that all-boy trip to Mt. Jefferson still hangs in my living room. Dad looks straight into the camera, his windblown hair as white as snow. My two tall brothers stand to his left. My son Ian is a gangly twelve-year-old. And above us all, the huge mountain looms like the memory of the one who is missing.

The September after my mother died, my father asked the men of the family to hike with him to Jefferson Park in her memory.

For my father, the best part of the wilderness was going back year after year at just the same time. Jefferson Park was his Brigadoon, an unchanging haven from the terrors of age in the world below.

I rebelled against this temporal tedium by resolving to visit Jefferson Park in a completely different season.

When my father turned 79 he canceled his September trip. The 10-mile hike had simply become too difficult for him. Would I be going anyway, he wondered?

In April, snowdrifts stop cars miles before there is enough snow to ski.

No, I told him, I'd rather try something new. I would ski there in winter. He raised his eyebrows.

As it turns out, Jefferson Park is much easier to visit in September than in early April, when I finally convinced two chums to join me on the ski trip. Not only is the park still buried by eight feet of snow in April, but the trailheads are under snow as well. The only plowed road is Highway 22, deep in the North Santiam canyon.

I calculated we would have to ski a total of 20 miles to visit Jefferson Park. The trip would require three days, carrying a winter tent and survival gear.

We loaded everything into my Subaru and drove up Forest Road 46 from Detroit until a big drift stopped us short. Ahead the snow was too patchy for skis, but too deep for tires. So we strapped our skis onto our backpacks and walked. After 3 awkward miles, alternately hiking and postholing through drifts, the snow was deep enough that we could put on our skis for good. Then we climbed another 6 arduous miles, constantly checking the map against the frozen terrain.

Shadows were lengthening when we finally crested Park Ridge, the 7000-foot guardian of Jefferson Park's northern rim. Mt. Jefferson loomed before us, its pink glaciers writhing in the sunset. Too exhausted to exclaim in wonder, we skied just far enough down the slope to escape the wind, dug out a flat circle in the snow, and set up our tent.

We set up our tent on the side of Park Ridge.

One of the advantages of snow camping is that you can put your tent almost anywhere. In summer Jefferson Park is so crowded that lakeshores are roped off for restoration. Good campsites are in demand, and rangers patrol for people who break the rules by camping within 100 feet of a lake.

In winter, if you want, you can camp on top of a lake.

The circular ledge we constructed for our campsite, using avalanche shovels and ski boots, was perched on the side of Park Ridge 400 feet above the park's plain. The view was great, but no one could possibly have pitched a tent there in summer.

The next day dawned blue, with a weird warm wind that soon had us stripped to shirtsleeves. We slathered on sunscreen, left most of our gear in the tent, and spent the day exploring Jefferson Park by ski. From the tracks we found, the only other visitors in the past six months had been coyotes, rabbits, and deer.

After a glorious day in the warm sun we returned to our campsite on Park Ridge to discover that our tent was gone.

How could our tent be gone? We had staked this domed structure into the snow with a dozen pegs, many of them scoop-shaped to hold snow. We had loaded the tent with our sleeping bags, pads, and extra gear.

We found nothing but an empty, circular snow platform. The tent and everything in it had disappeared.

We were 9 miles from our car. Night was approaching. We needed our tent.

Skiing across Park Ridge to Jefferson Park.

Could someone have stolen it?

There were no tracks of invaders. Besides, why would anyone ski in 9 miles, pack up our gear, and haul it away? If deranged thieves had lifted the tent away by helicopter, we would have heard an engine.

Increasingly desperate, we searched for clues.

On closer inspection, the site itself was not quite as we remembered. The tent's circular footprint was now six inches higher than the surrounding snow. Several stakes remained, lying loose on the surface of the snow.

Suddenly we realized what had happened.

The sun had been so hot that the entire snowpack had melted

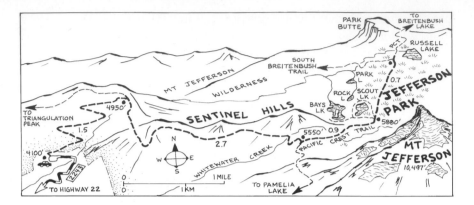

six inches during the day. The pegs had melted loose. Then even a small gust would have been able to send the dome tumbling down the slope.

We found the tent a few minutes later, with all our gear, where it had rolled into a grove of trees on Jefferson Park's plain.

A winter visit to Jefferson Park can be breathtaking, but it is fraught with hazards.

My father passed away at the age of 86. The University of Oregon recognized J. Wesley Sullivan posthumously with induction into the Hall of Achievement, the highest honor in Oregon journalism.

I honor him now, with the admission that there is a best time for everything. And the best time to visit Jefferson Park is in September.

Getting There: Three trailheads access Jefferson Park, but the easiest and most popular is on Whitewater Creek. It's usually open to hikers from mid-July to mid-October. To find it, drive 61 miles east of Salem on North Santiam Highway 22. Between mileposts 60 and 61 (beyond Detroit 10 miles or 21 miles north of the Santiam Y junction), turn left on Whitewater Road 2243. Follow this gravel route 7.4 miles to its end at a large parking area. Especially if you're leaving your car here overnight, leave no valuables inside and leave doors unlocked to discourage car clouters, an occasional problem here.

Hiking Tips: After 1.5 miles, turn right at a trail junction on a ridgecrest. At the 3.9-mile mark, a footbridge crosses Whitewater Creek. At the Pacific Crest Trail junction, turn left. For the next 0.9 mile the trailside meadows become larger and prettier until the path reaches Jefferson Park—where a confusion of trails proliferate. To follow the PCT, keep straight to the first glimpse of Scout Lake, then veer right. If you're backpacking, bring a stove, a permit, and the energy to seek out one of the remote, forested corners of the park for your camp.

Jefferson Park from Park Ridge in April.

OCTOBER
In Oregon

Jefferson Park in autumn.

WHY IT'S WHYCHUS

The Whychus Creek ford at Alder Springs.

S triped cliffs tower above Alder Springs, an oasis deep in the desert canyon of Whychus Creek. On a rock overhang nearby, red stick-figure petroglyphs remain from the ancients who lived here millennia ago.

The canyon is so quiet it's hard to believe you're just a few miles from the Central Oregon boomtown of Sisters.

The creek here was known as Squaw Creek until 2005. After local tribes complained that "squaw" had pejorative connotations, the label was switched to Whychus, a Sahaptin word for "a place to cross the water."

Once only diehard explorers could scramble to Alder Springs. An unusual land acquisition and a trail, however, have made the hike relatively easy. In fact, after walking 1.4 miles to Alder Springs, you'll probably have enough energy to hike another 1.6 miles to trail's end, at a bouldery rapids of the Deschutes River.

When I first described the route to Alder Springs in 1988, hikers had to cross a tumbleweed-strewn ranch on an ancient county right-of-way and then bushwhack a mile.

In the early 1990s a hermit bought the ranch and began putting up signs threatening people to keep their distance. Apparently he even chased some hikers away with a rifle. But the route through the ranch really was a public right-of-way, so a few brave explorers kept venturing to Alder Springs.

Finally one of those hikers discovered the real reason the hermit was so touchy. It turns out he had turned the old ranch house into a meth lab.

After a police raid, authorities confiscated the property and turned it over to the Crooked River National Grassland. That agency demolished

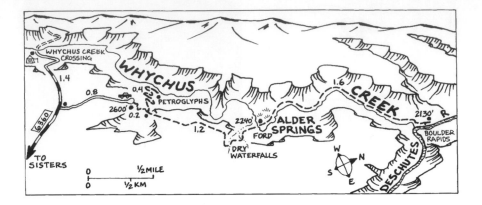

the house, tore out the barbed wire fences, and built a hiking trail.

Autumn is a pleasant time to hike this interesting trail, when the heat of summer has given way to crisp mornings and cool, clear afternoons. The trailhead perches on a rimrock plateau with views of Black Butte, Mt. Washington, and North Sister. Each June the rocky barrens here blooms with white death camas and pink bitterroot.

Getting There: Drive Highway 20 east from Santiam Pass to Sisters. On the far side of town, fork left toward Redmond on Highway 126 for 4.6 miles. Then turn left on Goodrich Road for 8.1 paved miles. Along the way the road zigzags and changes name, but keep going. When you reach a marker for milepost 7, turn left on gravel road 6360 and pass through a green gate. Follow this one-lane track 4.1 miles, turn right at an "Alder Springs" pointer, and take a rough gravel road 0.8 mile to a parking turnaround at road's end.

Hiking Tips: Bicycles and horses are not allowed. Dog owners are asked to bring a plastic bag to carry out dog waste. The entire area is closed from December 1 to March 31 each year to protect wildlife and soil.

The trail sets off downhill amid sparse junipers for a few hundred yards to a junction in a saddle. A side trail to the left descends 0.4 mile to a deadend at Whychus Creek's bank—but it's a worthwhile detour if you'd like to see the petroglyphs. To find them, look downstream at the base of a cliff, 40 feet from the creek. Don't touch these faint red markings! Unwise visitors have already damaged them by scratching them and attempting to wash them.

After visiting the petroglyphs, return to the junction and continue on the main trail 1.2 miles to a ford of Whychus Creek. You'll have to take off your shoes here because the creek is ankle deep in fall (and knee deep in spring), but it's seldom very cold.

OREGON FAVORITES

Long shadows at the Whychus Creek trailhead.   Below: Petroglyphs near the creek.

On the far shore, in a bend of the creek surrounded by gigantic cliffs, is Alder Springs—a lush grassy meadow with springs, a pond, and ponderosa pines. Camping is allowed here, but campfires are taboo and tents must be at least 50 feet from the trail or water.

If you're not yet ready to turn back, continue downstream another 1.6 miles to a rock outcrop overhanging a rapids of the raging Deschutes River. Half a dozen ponderosa pines cluster nearby. On the far shore, a jagged fin of striped palisades cuts the canyon slope like a serrated knife.

The trail ends at the uncrossable Deschutes. But it's a glorious spot for a picnic before heading back. And even after you've returned to your car you might yet explore a different part of Whychus Creek on your way home.

When you drive back to gravel Road 6360, turn right for 1.4 increasingly rough miles to Whychus Creek Crossing, a free, primitive campground. Park at the far end of the campground and walk onward 100 yards to a shallow, 20-foot-wide cave at the base of a cliff.

Here again you'll find the red petroglyphs of the mysterious hikers who traversed this desert canyon long ago.

SISTERS ROCKS

S urf rumbles through sea caves in the three monumental Sisters Rocks, the largest of a cluster of islands between two scenic, rarely visited beaches.

This state park on the Southern Oregon Coast between Port Orford and Gold Beach was purchased with Oregon Lottery money. Years ago, Oregon voters passed an initiative to dedicate a portion of lottery funds for parks and salmon. At first, legislators undercut that measure by reducing the state park budget to match the new lottery income. More recently, however, funds have been flowing for state parks after all.

If you drive Highway 101 past Sisters Rocks, you probably won't notice this park. There is a small state park sign, but it doesn't mention a name. The park itself is undeveloped.

Still, this part of the coast has a long history. Sisters Rocks served as a natural breakwater for the city of Frankport from 1893 to 1903. Rusting metal recalls a dock used to ship locally gathered tanoak bark to the S.H. Frank leather tannery in San Francisco. Sause Brothers Ocean Towing bought the old port in 1955 and quarried rock there until 1983.

Walk down the ancient road past a locked metal gate. Views extend north to Humbug Mountain and south to Cape Sebastian along beaches that rarely see footprints.

After 0.3 mile a left-hand fork of the road descends to Frankport Beach. The right-hand fork ends at a gravel plain between two of the monumental Sisters Rocks.

When you reach the first of the Sisters' semi-islands, scramble 100 feet up the slope straight ahead toward what looks like a crater. When you reach the crater's rim you'll discover it is actually the mouth of a giant sea cave.

Frankport Beach from Sisters Rocks.

183

The sea cave at Sisters Rocks has several entrances.   At right: Borax Hot Springs.

Two other entrances to this cave are around the left-hand side of the rock. Explore the tide pool area here at your own risk. Beware of slippery rocks and unexpected large waves.

Your entire visit to this state park is unlikely to require more than a mile of hiking or two hours of your time.

Sisters Rocks may not the biggest park on the coast, but with its secret sea cave, it may be one of the most fun to discover.

Getting There: Drive Highway 101 south of Port Orford 13 miles or north of Gold Beach 14 miles. Between mileposts 314 and 315 (and 1.3 miles south of Prehistoric Gardens' roadside dinosaur statues), look for the state park sign. Turn west beside a bluff on a very rough, rocky side road, and immediately park your car. If you have a global positioning system device, the location here is N42 35.73' W124 23.97'.

HOT SPRINGS OF THE HIGH DESERT

A chill descends on Oregon's high desert as winter approaches. But steam still wafts from a handful of hot springs — oases where a defiant summery warmth never fades.

A tour from Burns around Steens Mountain visits four of these natural springs. Three are free, and only one is off-limits for bathing. All are open year-round. Obviously southeast Oregon is a good place to soak in the scenery, even in winter.

Crane Hot Springs

From Burns, drive 25 miles east on Highway 78 to Crane Hot Springs, the first and only commercial hot springs on the tour.

At this unassuming ranch-style resort in the sagebrush flatlands of

Eastern Oregon, mineral-rich water boils out of the ground at 172 degrees Fahrenheit. By the time the water fills the resort's large open-air pond the temperature has dipped to a more modest 90 to 100 degrees. In the adjacent hot tub rooms, however, you can crank up the heat as high as you like.

After a swim, you could camp in Crane Hot Springs' campground, but it's a little stark. Each of the cabins available here has a double bed and a hide-a-bed. There's no TV or phone, and bathrooms are outside down a boardwalk.

If you're looking for posher digs, plan to drive back to Burns for the night. The Sage Country Bed & Breakfast Inn is a 1907 Georgian-Colonial home on a full block in downtown Burns. Decorated with antiques, the inn provides guests a full breakfast.

Mickey Hot Springs

The moonscape at Mickey Hot Springs includes boiling pools, steam jets, mudpots, and the scalding, 30-foot-deep Morning Glory Pool. The view stretches across desert hills to the snowy ridge of Steens Mountain.

Deep in the desert on gravel back roads, this hot springs is in an undesignated wilderness, so it can be hard to find. All of the natural pools here are too hot for humans, but bathers have carved one bathtub-sized basin where water cools to a bearable temperature.

Be warned there are no railings to keep visitors from the brink of boiling pools, so this is not a good place to bring pets or children.

Alvord Hot Springs

This unmarked spa features a dramatic view of Oregon's driest spot, the Alvord Desert. The desert's 9-mile alkali playa receives just six inches of annual precipitation, so skies are almost always blue.

The springs fill two 8-by-8-foot concrete pools at about 102 degrees Fahrenheit. Visitors are asked to bring no glass containers and to carry out any litter.

A boiling creek runs through Mickey Hot Springs.

Although the hot springs are generally open to the public, the land is actually owned by the private Alvord Ranch. Don't be surprised if the rancher drives by and asks for a $5 fee.

After soaking in Alvord Hot Springs, you could set up a tent in the unmarked Pike Creek Camp-

Alvord Hot Springs overlooks the desert.

ground. To find it, drive 2 miles north on the main gravel road, turn left across a yellow cattle guard, and bump up a rough side road 0.6 mile.

If the weather's too iffy to camp, drive south on the main paved

Getting There: From Burns, drive 25 miles east on Highway 78 to **Crystal Crane Hot Springs**, the first and only commercial hot springs on the tour. The facilities are open from 9am to 9pm Monday through Saturday, and 1pm to 9pm on Sundays. Expect to pay about $3.50 for an all-day pass to the pond, and $7.50 per person for an hour in the hot tubs. If you're camping, a $15 fee includes access to showers. The resort also offers five flat-roofed, one-room cabins that rent for about $50 for two. In Burns, the Sage Country Bed & Breakfast Inn (541-573-7243 or www.sagecoun-tryinn.com) at 350½ W. Monroe Street charges about $100 for a room for two, including a full breakfast.

To find **Mickey Hot Springs** from Crystal Crane Hot Springs, drive south-east away from Burns on Highway 78 another 41 miles. At a pointer for Fields near milepost 65, turn right on a paved road. After 31.5 miles, im-mediately before the first of two 90-degree corners, turn left across a green cattle guard onto an unmarked gravel side road. (If you reach the Alvord Ranch, you've driven 5 miles too far.) Follow this washboard gravel track through several zigzags for 2.6 miles, keep left at a fork, and after another 3.9 miles park at a railed turnaround for the hot springs on the right.

To find **Alvord Hot Springs** from Mickey Hot Springs, return 6.5 miles to the main paved road and continue south 10.5 miles toward Fields. Beyond the Alvord Ranch 5.7 miles, look for the hot springs' tin shed 200 yards to the left of the road.

To find **Borax Hot Springs**, start at the desert hamlet of Fields. Drive north on paved Highway 205 toward Frenchglen for 1.3 miles. When you reach a junction, go straight onto the paved road that leads north to High-way 78. After 0.4 mile, turn right beside a power substation onto a dirt road that follows a large powerline. At the first fork (after 2.1 miles) veer left away from the powerline for 1.8 miles and park beside a closed wire gate with a warning sign. Then hike north and east a mile on old roads to Borax Lake and the unswimmable hot springs pools beyond.

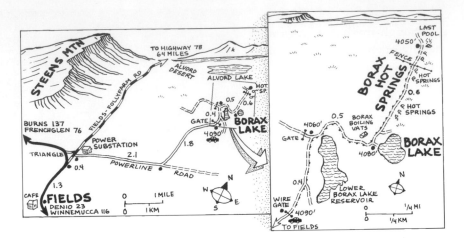

road for 23 miles to Fields. This remote roadside settlement consists of a combination cafe, store, motel, garage, and gas station. Other than the cafe's hamburgers and milkshakes, there isn't much to recommend in

Fields. It is, however, just a few miles from the next stop on the hot springs tour.

Borax Hot Springs

At Borax Hot Springs, fish thrive in warm alkaline water.

During the wetter climate of the Ice Age, a gigantic lake filled the valley east of Steens Mountain hundreds of feet deep, spilling north to the Snake River. As the rains lessened, the lake evaporated.

Incredibly, not all of the fish perished. At Borax Lake, one minnow-like species evolved to survive in the increasingly warm, salty water. Today the Borax chub lives in 600-foot-wide Borax Lake, and nowhere else on earth.

Borax Lake fell into private hands in the late 1800s, when entrepreneurs hired Chinese laborers to collect sodium borate crusts and dissolve them in huge vats to produce borax. Mule-drawn wagon caravans hauled the chalky borax more than a hundred miles to the railroad in Winnemucca.

The non-profit Nature Conservancy bought the lake and

OREGON FAVORITES

Algae at Borax Hot Springs (above and lower left) feed endangered fish. Metal boiling tubs remain (opposite) from efforts to extract borax from the alkaline lake.

adjacent hot springs in the 1990s to preserve the area's fragile ecosystem. Swimming is banned, and dogs are not allowed, even on leash. Still, it's worth hiking through the area to see the colorful hot spring vents and the rusted remains of the old borax vats beside the lake.

At the trailhead a sign warns, "Danger! Hot Springs. Scalding Water. Ground May Collapse. Control Children and Pets."

Heeding these cautions, hike onward along the road. Ignore a side road to the right after 0.2 mile and another road to the left after 0.4 mile. You'll pass a lower reservoir and the old boiling vats before climbing up to Borax Lake.

Dozens of smaller hot springs, strung out in a line to the north for 0.6 mile, are visible from here as wisps of steam rising from the grass. For a closer look, walk back 100 feet toward the vats, turn right on a faint road, and keep straight toward distant Steens Mountain.

The pools are to the right of the road, but be careful if you leave the track, because these deep, sheer-sided springs are dangerously hot. After half a mile a fence crosses the road. Beyond the fence 200 yards, where the road veers left, pause at two large, final hot spring pools on the right before turning back toward your car.

To complete your tour around Steens Mountain, take Highway 205 northwest for 50 miles to the tiny village of Frenchglen.

Then it's an hour's drive back to Burns through the Malheur National Wildlife Refuge. In October, great flocks of birds stop here on their migration south.

The high desert can be a silent, lonely place. But there is a stark beauty in that solitude—and there are islands of warmth, for those who know where to look.

45 FORGOTTEN IRISH MOUNTAIN

Irish Mountain may be the least known peak on Oregon's Cascade crest.

I'm willing to bet that more people have summited all Three Sisters than have found their way to the top of this 6893-foot crag north of Waldo Lake. To find out why, I recently led a group from the Obsidians outdoor club on a backpacking trip to Irish Mountain.

We came back without an explanation.

We hiked 5.3 miles to Irish Mountain's base on a reasonable trail and camped at a swimmable alpine lake. The next day we scrambled to the summit in 40 minutes. Views extended south across Waldo Lake to Mt. Thielsen and north past the Three Sisters to Mt. Hood.

Apparently Irish Mountain isn't famous because — well, because it just isn't famous.

Admittedly, the season for visiting this remote southern corner of the

Three Sisters Wilderness is not long. Snow covers the trail until mid-July. August is abuzz with mosquitoes. But autumn can be delightful, with fields of ripe huckleberries in September.

As the huckleberry leaves turn scarlet in October, the risk of winter weather also increases. Bring proper gear and don't hike alone, especially if you're venturing here late in the season.

The trailhead for Irish Mountain is the same one that hikers

From the Irish Mountain Trail (below), you have to scramble half a mile to the summit benchmark (above), where views extend across Waldo Lake to Diamond Peak (opposite).

use for the popular, nearly level walk to the Erma Bell Lakes.

The trail starts with a footbridge across Skookum Creek. The word *skookum* means "powerful" in Chinook jargon, the old trade language of Northwest Indians, and accurately describes this roaring stream.

After 0.6 mile on an easy, broad trail through old-growth woods with rhododendron bushes, fork uphill to the left on the smaller Irish Mountain Trail.

In another half a mile you'll reach forest-rimmed Otter Lake, a 10-acre pool that may have otters, and certainly has fish.

The trail skirts Otter Lake for 0.4 mile, crosses the inlet creek, and then forks again. Most hikers go right, setting out on an 8-mile loop that returns to the trailhead via the Erma Bell Lakes. But if you're headed for Irish Mountain, keep left.

Now the path becomes a little faint from lack of use. The tree blazes along this route look upside down, shaped like exclamation points instead of like the letter "i". In the early days of the Forest Service, rangers used "i" markings to indicate regular trails, while exclamation points signified "ways" — rougher, steeper routes.

From Otter Lake the Irish Mountain Trail climbs a ridge for 1.8 miles. Then it follows a crest through huckleberry patches for a mile to a 100-foot

pond. Regular trail maintenance ends here, so expect to step over a few small logs for the final mile to Irish Mountain's base.

When you reach a heather plateau at the 5.1-mile mark you'll finally see Irish Mountain

A nameless off-trail lake on the north flank of Irish Mountain overlooks the Three Sisters.

193

The east face of Irish Mountain towers above a pond near the Pacific Crest Trail.

Getting There: From Interstate 5 just south of Eugene, take exit 188 and follow Highway 58 toward Oakridge 31 miles. Before Oakridge, opposite the Middle Fork Ranger Station, turn left at a sign for Westfir. When you reach this village in 2 miles, continue straight on Aufderheide Road 19 for another 25.6 paved miles. Just before the rentable Box Canyon Guard Station, turn right on gravel Road 1957 for 4 miles to its end at primitive Skookum Campground.

ahead, a forested ridge topped by rocky crags. The plateau has been so severely scoured by Ice Age glaciers that the exposed bedrock still shows the scratch marks left by rocks dragged beneath the ice.

After crossing the plateau for 0.2 mile the trail passes between two charming little lakes. They're only a few hundred feet long, but were plenty deep enough for our group to go swimming.

There are plenty of flat spots to camp near the two lakes, but so few people visit that we didn't find campfire rings. We didn't build a ring of rocks either. These days, backpackers are encouraged to cook on stoves, and use campfires only in emergencies.

Beyond the two small lakes the trail becomes almost unfindable — and it doesn't lead to Irish Mountain's summit anyway.

If you have some route-finding skills, leave the trail at the two small lakes and strike off through the open woods, heading uphill to the southeast. It's easy to find Irish Mountain, but there are three summits, so it can be tricky to find the right one.

The trail starts by crossing Skookum Creek.

Of the three summits, the big brown cinder pyramid to the north is the least interesting. The crag to the south is not the highest point either. Instead head for the south side of the middle crag. Even here you will have to use your hands for a few feet as you scramble along lava cliffs.

The summit has two US Geological Survey markers, one of them from 1916. Far to the north, Mt. Hood is a white dwarf on the left shoulder of Mt. Jefferson. To the east, Cultus Lake shines in the Central Oregon sun.

After the exhilaration of this summit, I led our Obsidian group on a bushwhacking tour around the mountain's north flank. In four miles, ambling through the open woods, we passed 17 lakes and 19 ponds. Lakes, we decided, were large enough that it would be possible to swim in them.

Of the 17 lakes we found on our off-trail exploration around Irish Mountain, only one appeared to have fish. Even the ponds, however, had clusters of blue and purple dragonflies zooming about.

Irish Mountain is one of the ten tallest peaks in Lane County. It's the highest point of the Cascade Range for 30 miles.

But it's forgotten, and I can't figure out why.

A plateau with heather meadows and small lakes abuts Irish Mountain on the west.

NOVEMBER
In Oregon

Sunset Bay at Shore Acres.

The light display in Shore Acres' gardens opens each winter on Thanksgiving (photo by Shirley Bridgham).

LIGHTS AT SHORE ACRES

Groundskeepers insist that "something's blooming every day of the year" at Shore Acres State Park, on the rugged coast west of Coos Bay. From Thanksgiving to New Year's Day, more than a quarter million lights decorate the formal clifftop gardens as well.

But the gardens are not the only reason to plan a stroll along this stretch of Oregon's shore. The park is also haunted by the history of one of Oregon's wealthiest families. And just beyond the prim flower beds is wild scenery of the first order. Gigantic breakers off the North Pacific explode against tilted sandstone cliffs. Sea lions bark from whitecapped reefs.

North Bend timber baron Louis Simpson bought this dramatic seaside estate as a Christmas surprise for his wife in 1906. Today Simpson's mansion is gone, but a portion of the Oregon Coast Trail traces the shore past the grand old estate's gardens.

To try a stroll through the history here, leave your car at the far end of the state park's lot and walk across oceanfront lawns to a small observation building perched on a cliff.

So far you'll have walked only a few hundred feet, but it's almost precisely the same route explored by Louis J. Simpson in 1905 on his first visit. Simpson was overseeing one of his many timber cruising crews when he saw a glint of ocean through the trees and decided to take a closer look.

"It was perfect day and the sun was shining gloriously," Simpson later recalled. "I determined to work my way down to the headland to see what the view might be like. I did have to crawl on my hands and knees through . . . the densest undergrowth you ever saw outside of the tropics. Finally, hot and breathless, I emerged on a little open space. Immediately I saw what a place for a country home!"

The view today is still inspiring. During winter storms, forty-foot waves pound the bluff below the observation building. The surf is slowly grinding the tilted sandstone strata into a series of weirdly stepped reefs.

Louis Simpson built his summer mansion right where the little observation building now stands. Styled after homes he had seen in Massachusetts, the shake-covered building featured bay windows and an enormous pillared porch that faced the ocean. The entry hall was richly paneled with Oregon myrtlewood and lit with specially ordered Tiffany lamps.

Louis Simpson could never have afforded such a posh retreat if it had not been for his father Asa, the man who amassed the Simpson fortune. Born a humble farmer's son in Maine, Asa Simpson learned the shipbuilding trade and sailed to California with his two brothers in time for the Gold Rush. He opened a lumberyard and sent his two brothers to scout sawmill sites along the Pacific Coast. Both brothers died during those voyages. One brother's ship capsized with a load of timber on the Columbia

Although Louis Simpson's mansion burned, a caretaker cottage remains in the gardens.

River bar. The second brother's ship wrecked while bringing sawmill machinery across Coos Bay's bar.

Asa salvaged the equipment from the Coos Bay wreck in 1856 and opened a mill nearby at what is now North Bend. To reduce the risk of shipwrecks like the ones that killed his brothers, he bought a steam tugboat that could tow sailing ships across the treacherous bar in relative safety. Then he built a Coos Bay shipyard that began turning out a two-masted freighter every nine months. The finest of these ships, the three-masted schooner *Western Shore*, broke all records in 1875 by sailing from Astoria around Cape Horn to Ireland with a full load of 1800 tons of Oregon wheat in just 101 days.

Simpson asked his ship captains to bring back exotic plants for his estate's gardens.

Asa's son Louis grew up amid luxury. The family owned palatial homes in both Stockton and Oakland, and often traveled to the East Coast and Europe, collecting fine art. Louis studied briefly at the University of California in Berkeley. Still, he had almost no business training when he was given charge of the family's Coos Bay operations in 1899 at the age of 21.

When Louis arrived at North Bend, the white buildings of the Simpson Company lined the bay, but he noticed that the woods behind were undeveloped. Because his father still dictated every detail of work at the shipyard and sawmill, Louis decided to save up his salary to undertake a different kind of enterprise. In 1902 he borrowed $25,000, bought up the nearby land, platted a townsite, established a post office, and incorporated the city of North Bend. He was promptly elected mayor — hardly surprising, given that he owned all but two of the town's lots. Then he wrote his father that he was raising the rent on land the company had been using.

Furious, Asa took the next ship to North Bend to browbeat his upstart son. But Louis didn't budge.

Within a year Louis had built a city he could call his own. He sold lots to company workers and to ambitious entrepreneurs from the entire Pacific Coast. He raised capital to open an iron works, ice factory, hotel, gas works, milk condensing plant, door factory, and woolen mill. He donated land for a public dock and for Mercy Hospital. Later he helped organize

Simpson Cove is a short walk from the formal gardens.

the Bank of Oregon.

While riding the crest of these business successes, Louis married Cassie Hendricks and presented her with the Shore Acres mansion as a Christmas gift. The Simpsons' country home became the scene of parties and gay summer gatherings for the social elite of both California and Oregon. Guests often arrived on Simpson ships to stay for weeks.

Gradually Louis made the summer estate grander and grander. In 1914 he added an enormous wing to the mansion with a 52-foot, heated indoor swimming pool in the style of a Roman bath. A Palm Room connected the addition to the main house. Upstairs were still more bedrooms and a new, 76-by-36-foot ballroom. A Chinese cook and three servants kept the estate in order.

North of the house stood a two-story carriage house and a path to two concrete tennis courts. South of the house, beyond the private beach at Simpson Cove, Louis added a fifteen-cow dairy farm that also supplied the estate with vegetables, chickens, and eggs. He cleared the forest near the house and hired crews to build four acres of formal gardens, including a Japanese garden pool lined with boulders hoisted up with horse teams from Simpson Cove.

To continue your tour of the estate's grounds, turn left along the cliff edge from the observation building. Then veer left into the fabulous formal gardens. Simpson's ship captains brought exotic plants from around

the world to fill the beds. Today only a few Monterey pines, cypresses, and fruit trees remain from those original gardens. The new plantings feature 22 varieties of rhododendrons and azaleas.

And yes, you really can find flowers blooming even in November. Late fall bloomers include penstemons, begonias, fuchsias, some roses, and a showy South African ornamental named red-hot poker.

Walk through the boxwood hedges' geometric designs, circle the Japanese garden's pool, and return to the paved oceanfront trail. Then turn left for a quarter mile down to the beach at Simpson Cove, a broad triangle of sand embraced by ochre cliffs. For a longer hike, continue on an unpaved path along the ocean bluffs to a viewpoint of Simpson Reef and Shell Island, where sea lions lounge and bark. This makes a good turnaround point for your day's trip.

The turnaround point for Louis Simpson's fortunes came after a spectacular peak in World War I. The war had revived the sagging demand for the Simpson Company's wooden ships and lumber. When Asa Simpson died in Oakland in 1915, Louis became sole ruler of the company's empire. He brought a shipload of the family's European art treasures to Shore Acres, including marble statues and copies of oils by Italian masters. In 1916 he moved his family from North Bend to Shore Acres, making the mansion their year-round home.

To cap off his success, Louis entered the race for governor, inviting the newspaper editors of Oregon to help kick off his bid with a luncheon bash at Shore Acres. How could he lose? The debonair six-term mayor of North Bend, known throughout the state as the "handsome stranger," was active in the state's YMCA and Elks club. He ran on a populist Democratic platform to develop Oregon and to extend the state's new women's suffrage law nationwide.

But Simpson did lose the governor's race, and within days World War I ended, canceling demand for wooden ships. In 1920, his wife died of kidney failure at Shore Acres. Suddenly his world was crumbling.

As you hike back from the sea lion viewpoint you'll be following in the hurried footsteps of Louis Simpson on the night his dream home went up in flames. No one knows why Louis was out walking here near the dairy farm at 2am on the morning of the Fourth of July, 1921. But when he noticed a glow on the horizon to the north he raced down the dark trail to Simpson Cove and sprinted through the formal garden paths. The mansion was already engulfed by the fire. By dawn, it was gone. No one had been hurt, but all of the house's artworks and all of his company's records were lost.

Insurance paid only half of the fire's loss. Louis moved temporarily into the caretakers' cottage that still remains beside the formal gardens. Later that year he married a second wife, Lela. Two years later, when one of his company's schooners wrecked on Simpson Reef, dumping three million board feet of lumber onto the shore here, he tried to make the best of tragedy by salvaging the wood for construction of a new mansion on the ashes of the old. Plain but huge, the great shingled barracks that began to rise in 1927 was 224 feet long, with two stories and 17 rooms.

Work stopped on the new mansion, however, when the stock market crash of 1929 staggered Simpson's fortunes yet again. He moved into the shell of the uncompleted house, hastily finishing a few of the rooms. In 1932 he donated 134 acres south of the estate for Cape Arago State Park.

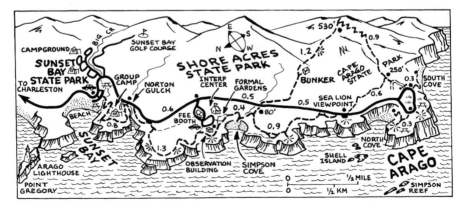

Getting There: From Highway 101 in Coos Bay, follow "Shore Acres" signs 9 miles to Charleston, and then continue straight 4 miles. A mile past Sunset Bay State Park, turn right into the Shore Acres entrance, and park by the oceanfront lawns at the far end of the parking area. Expect a fee of $5 per car. Dogs are not allowed in the park.

Hours: The park is usually open from 8am to sunset, but from Thanksgiving through New Years Day it stays open until 9:30pm, and the light displays are turned on at 4pm.

In September, 1936, a wildfire swept toward Shore Acres. The Simpsons fled to North Bend. Although the mansion survived the fire, most of the outbuildings were lost and the family never returned. On December 10, 1942, he sold the remaining 637 acres of the Shore Acres estate, including the rambling second mansion, to the state of Oregon for a mere $29,000. The Army converted the house to a barracks for troops guarding the Southern Oregon coast. Then it fell into disuse.

Meanwhile, Louis Simpson's long-time business competitor from Coos Bay, Ben Chandler, had become chairman of the State Highway Commission that oversaw state parks. Sensing an opportunity to score a symbolic victory over his rival, Chandler ordered Simpson's run-down mansion destroyed in December, 1948. Louis J. Simpson died three weeks later in a small Barview cottage near North Bend.

Today, with half a million visitors a year touring the old Shore Acres estate, parks officials have begun to regret Chandler's vindictive decision. Together with the Friends of Shore Acres, the Department of Parks and Recreation has been discussing ways to rebuild the original 1906 Simpson mansion. The enormous cost is just one of many obstacles that still lie in the project's path.

But even without the old mansion, the spirit of the Simpson family seems to linger here like a sea mist. Walking through the festively lit gardens on a winter's evening, you can almost hear the distant laughter of the Simpson's wealthy party guests. Then the surf crashes with a renewed roar, and the laughter is lost.

The gardens' gazebo is popular for weddings.

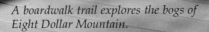

47
TRUE GRIT AT EIGHT DOLLAR MOUNTAIN

A boardwalk trail explores the bogs of Eight Dollar Mountain.

Paul Brown never met John Wayne, but Brown also knows the meaning of true grit.

Brown battled a crippling genetic disease while helping to turn Wayne's favorite Oregon hangout into a nature study and research center.

Today the Siskiyou Field Institute offers classes on natural history and outdoor lore at its 850-acre Deer Creek Center. The center sprawls at the base of Eight Dollar Mountain, a cone-shaped peak 20 miles southwest of Grants Pass. An easy hike nearby leads to one of the world's largest stands of Darlingtonia, a bog pitcher plant that catches insects.

In the early 1980s the property was a private ranch. John Wayne liked to visit the place so much that he stabled a horse there. Locals say he sometimes showed up at the bar in the nearby village of Selma.

At about the same time, Paul Brown was studying park management at a California college. On a whim, he answered an ad to staff a Forest Service cabin for the summer at Store Gulch, a remote canyon along the Illinois River a few miles west of Eight Dollar Mountain.

Paul Brown points out a Darlingtonia *plant at a bog near the Deer Creek Center.*

The ad didn't mention that the previous staffer at Store Gulch had just been murdered. Brown found that out when he arrived at the tiny shack at the edge of the Kalmiopsis Wilderness.

"Didn't they tell you?" the Forest Service man asked Brown when he arrived. The previous caretaker had been stabbed by drug users who then swam the river and lit out into the wilderness.

That summer as a caretaker at the cabin, Brown had to deal with hippie survivalists and reclusive gold miners. One man briefly held him at gunpoint on a suspension footbridge high above the river, complaining about government regulations.

But Brown also had time to explore the Klamath Mountains. He fell in love with the green-pooled rivers, red rock canyons, and strange forests of Jeffrey pines and Port Orford cedars.

For the next fifteen years Brown worked in Silicon Valley as an art director for advertising and consulting companies. When illness forced him to retire three years ago—he suffers from a congenital pancreatic condition that causes great pain—he thought about returning to the

Beside Eight Dollar Mountain, a ranch once popular with John Wayne has become an environmental study center.

Southern Oregon wilds.

Once again, Brown answered an ad for a caretaker. This time, he would be staying at the ranch John Wayne liked on Deer Creek at Eight Dollar Mountain.

The ranch had seen hard times. John Wayne's friend had sold it to people who let it become rundown. When the Deer Creek property came on the market again, the Siskiyou Field Institute bought it and signed up Paul Brown.

Allied with the Southern Oregon University Foundation and the Siskiyou Field Institute, the Deer Creek Center is a nonprofit group dedicated to studying the natural history of the Klamath-Siskiyou range. An anonymous $1 million donation enabled the group to buy the ranch and start developing the education and research center.

Brown agreed to work without pay in exchange for the use of a small apartment in the property's ranch house.

One of his first jobs was to help an Americorps staffer and volunteer youth groups clean up the garbage the previous owners had left behind. The debris filled eleven Dumpster trailers.

The Deer Creek Center left the ranch's living room largely unchanged, and acknowledges Wayne's influence with a touch of humor.

For the next three years, Brown assisted the contractors and the paid staffers who created the education center.

They converted a meeting room in a large garage to a classroom and laboratory. They built a picnic pavilion and a solar-heated shower house, allowing two acres of lawn to serve as a campground for visiting students. They set up two yurts as dormitories, each with room for ten or more students.

The huge ranch house itself was left much as it was when John Wayne stayed there. The living room, with a vaulted ceiling and hand-carved wooden beams, opens onto a flagstone patio. The view stretches across a mile of

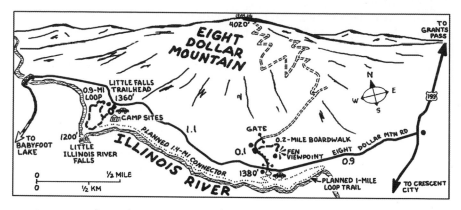

pasture, now leased to an organic dairy. Two bedrooms and a dorm room in the ranch house are available for students and instructors to rent.

All the time that Brown was fixing up the house, building trails, and assisting instructors, he was also struggling with the pain of his disease.

He had become used to pain. The year before he started work at the Deer Creek Center he had mistaken the onset of appendicitis for another pancreatic attack. When his agony finally became unbearable, he drove himself to a hospital. He managed to stagger inside before passing out in the emergency room.

The doctor who treated him was astonished to discover that Brown's appendix had burst three days earlier.

Brown survived that bout with appendicitis, and later a failed gallbladder, but his pancreatic disease continued to worsen. Finally, at the age of 49, Brown retired from his volunteer job at Deer Creek and moved to a city apartment, closer to medical help.

Getting There: To find the Deer Creek Center from Grants Pass, drive 20 miles south on Highway 199 to the flashing yellow light in Selma, turn right on Illinois River Road 1.4 miles, and veer left to a parking area by the ranch house.

Many of the Siskiyou Field Institute's courses are held in spring and summer. Classes in fall and winter often include mushroom identification and wilderness first aid. For details, including tuition and lodging rates, check *www.thesfi.org* or call 541-597-8530.

To explore Eight Dollar Mountain on the boardwalk trail, drive back to Selma and turn south on Highway 199 for 4 miles. At milepost 24, turn right on Eight Dollar Road for 0.9 mile to a marked gravel parking area on the left. Walk up a paved road to the right 200 yards to find the start of the 0.2-mile boardwalk.

The Deer Creek Center that Paul Brown helped create is part of a larger effort to preserve Eight Dollar Mountain.

Amost perfectly conical, the 3-mile-wide mountain looks like a volcano, but is actually an erosional remnant that includes some of Oregon's oldest rocks. The reddish peridotite and greenish serpentine here began as seafloor rock more than 200 million years ago. These rocks produce a soil so infertile that plants have struggled to adapt.

As a result, Eight Dollar Mountain is an island of botanical diversity, home to odd bogs and an astonishing variety of rare flowers.

With the purchase of 650 acres by the Oregon Parks and Recreation Department, all of Eight Dollar Mountain is now in public or nonprofit ownership. Recreation plans for the area are still uncertain, although there has been talk of building an 8-mile loop trail around the peak.

In the meantime, the two best ways to explore the area are to sign up for a class at the Deer Creek Center or to hike a boardwalk trail to a viewpoint.

The pitcher plant (Darlingtonia) catches insects for fertilizer, making up for the area's nutrient-poor soil.

The landscape you will see from the short boardwalk path is strange in many ways. Although Eight Dollar Mountain receives more than 60 inches of rain a year, the rock has so few nutrients that pine trees here are sparse and stunted. At first glance some slopes resemble a desert.

The mountain is so conical that it has virtually no creeks. Instead runoff oozes downhill through vast fens, boggy slopes punctuated with the baseball-bat shapes of pitcher plants.

It takes true grit for plants to survive on Eight Dollar Mountain. This wild corner of Oregon also seems to attract men of grit: John Wayne and Paul Brown.

48

THE TREASURE OF HAYRICK BUTTE

From the lodge at Hoodoo Ski Bowl, Hayrick Butte's rock mesa appears inaccessible.

Climbing Hayrick Butte with skis is one of those stupid challenges that seem to fascinate only a select group of idiots like me. Blame it on our genes.

Even if the name "Hayrick Butte" means nothing to you, you've probably seen this half-mile-long plateau. It's right next to Hoodoo Butte at Santiam Pass.

Hoodoo Butte's cinder cone looks a big haystack. No one knows exactly how Hoodoo got its name. But beside it, flat-topped Hayrick Butte must have reminded pioneers of a gigantic hayrick—a rack for drying hay.

Entirely surrounded by cliffs, the 500-foot-tall plateau is a remnant of a large lava flow that once covered the Santiam Pass area. Ice Age glaciers scraped away most of the rock, but apparently couldn't get a purchase on this chunk.

For years the cliffs defended Hayrick Butte as effectively as the wall of a Crusader castle. For years, no one cared.

Climbers weren't interested in scaling a flat-topped butte, especially

Even at a gap in the cliffs on Hayrick Butte's east face, the final pitch is nearly vertical.

when spire-topped Mt. Washington is waiting nearby. Skiers shunned the butte, considering it needlessly suicidal when Hoodoo offers a perfectly good ski area next door.

Then someone placed two geocaches on top of Hayrick Butte.

Geocaching is a modern-day treasure hunt, using GPS (global positioning system) devices.

In olden times, a pirate might have filled a treasure chest with booty, buried it in a remote spot, and marked a cryptic map with an X to puzzle future searchers.

The modern geocacher puts a few trinkets in a Tupperware container or ammunition can, conceals it in a publicly accessible spot, and posts the GPS coordinates on the Internet to challenge adventurers.

One popular website for the sport, *geocaching.com,* lists more than a million active geocache sites worldwide. People who plant caches are supposed to get permission from land owners, so most sites are in parks or on other public land.

To join the treasure hunt you need a handheld GPS device or a GPS-enabled mobile phone. Then you choose a place that interests you from a website, enter the coordinates, and follow your device.

It's a fun way to fill an afternoon with a hike to a new and often unexpectedly cool destination. Once you've found the cache you can sign its logbook and keep some of its treasure—as long as you leave something of equal or greater value in its place. It's also good manners to put the box back exactly where you found it.

Finding the cache can be trickier than you'd think. GPS devices are not accurate at close range, so you'll be on your own for the last few yards. Often the boxes are cunningly concealed in hollow trees or behind rocks.

Worse, some geocachers put boxes in crazy places, like the top of Hayrick Butte.

I'm sure I would have been able to resist Hayrick Butte, but a guy sent me an email complaining that he hadn't been able get there. He'd scrambled along the entire western side of Hayrick Butte and had found nothing but cliffs. Had the geocacher dropped a box there from a helicopter, he wondered?

I didn't think so. I suspected there was a gap on the east side.

In retrospect, I think my "stupid guy" gene had kicked in.

I'd already been planning a ski trip with two buddies to try out our new overnight snow expedition gear. They wanted a tough test with full packs. I was surprised how easily they agreed to my suggestion that we head for the east face of Hayrick Butte.

The starting point for our trek was the Benson Sno-Park, just off the Hoodoo entrance road at Santiam Pass. This parking loop is popular with Nordic skiers, snowshoers, and snowmobilers alike. If you go, be sure to bring a sno-park permit, available at ski shops and outdoor stores.

In the middle of the Benson Sno-Park loop there's a big log-walled warm-up cabin and a building with restrooms.

From the sno-park, separate routes lead out for motorized and non-motorized snow travelers. The most popular goals are four log shelters with mountain views and woodstoves. Maps and signs mark the trails.

Dave Reuter at a view of Mt. Washington.

Hayrick Butte looms like a battleship a quarter mile from the sno-park, so it's pretty hard to miss. The first few hundred yards of the route are actually flat. Then we crossed a snowmobile road and started to climb through mountain hemlock woods.

Skis are pretty much useless in a steep forest full of tree wells. One of our guys had thought to bring snowshoes, which worked for a while. But snowshoes don't do well on side slopes. Your only choice is to walk straight uphill. Before long we were all post-holing up the snow, pulling ourselves from tree to tree and branch to branch.

Scaling a slope this steep with skis strapped to your backpack is like swimming uphill with a dead kangaroo.

Finally we built a staircase in a sort of snow tunnel, and passed the packs up, one at a time.

We set up an expedition tent for practice.

And then we were on top, sweating and panting from the climb.

At first the top of Hayrick Butte seemed a lot like the bottom—a big flat area with woods and openings.

Only after we had eaten lunch and set out around the rim did we discover the magic of this island in the sky. Whichever direction you choose, you soon are stopped by a cliff edge with breathtaking views. At one corner you face Mt. Jefferson, a white pyramid in the wilderness. Next you dead end at an overlook of frozen Big Lake. Then it's Hoodoo, Mt. Washington, or Black Butte.

A snowy field near the plateau's southeast tip confounded us with a strange, funnel-shaped chasm. Warm air rose from a 30-foot-deep hole in the ground.

We circled the hole warily before deciding it must be the mouth of a lava tube. The cave must have another entrance on the flank of Hayrick Butte, and draw warmer air up from the pass below.

We were tired. We set up the expedition tent we had brought, just for practice. Then we packed up, completed our circuit of the rim to make sure there was no easier way down, took off our skis, and followed our footsteps down the east face of Hayrick Butte.

When I got home my wife Janell asked, "So what was in the geocache?"

I looked at her blankly.

"You know, the geocache on top of Hayrick Butte. That's why you climbed up there, isn't it?"

I frowned. "Right. I forgot about the cache."

"So then you're going back to find it?"

"No! Definitely not."

Janell watched me, waiting for the stupid guy gene to kick in.

"Well, maybe," I said. "Yes."

*After circling the butte we
decided there was no easier way down.*

December
In Oregon

Lookout at
Warner Mountain

The fanciest rental fire lookout in Oregon is also the most difficult to access.

Expect to ski or snowshoe as much as 10 miles, gaining up to a grueling 2400 feet of elevation, to reach the elegant Warner Mountain Lookout, between Oakridge and Diamond Peak.

Judging from the guest log entries, about a third of the groups that rent this panoramic cabin underestimate the difficulty of the trip and set out so late in the day that they arrive by flashlight.

Atop a 41-foot tower, the lookout was built in 1986 as a modernized replica of the cute "cupola-style" lookouts from the 1920s. The 14-by-14-foot cabin has a pull-down ladder in-side that accesses a smaller observa-tion story where staffers use a fire locator table to spot smoke plumes during the summer fire season.

49

Because roads aren't plowed to the rental lookout tower, you may have to ski as much as 10 miles.

There is no water, but it's easy to melt snow on the cabin's propane heater.

The lookout is available as a rental from November to mid-May, when it's not needed for fire detection. At either end of that rental season the snow pack is light enough that guests generally can drive within 3 or 4 miles of the lookout. The rest of winter, snow blocks the access road 6 to 10 miles from the tower.

"The orange glow of the tower, hidden in a sea of white snow, in the dark, was a huge relief," wrote one visitor in the guest book after skiing five hours in the dark to find the cabin.

"When we reached the door the lock had ice hanging off of it and was completely frozen. The warm fire inside" (of the cabin's thermostat-controlled propane woodstove) "was taunting us through the window while the wind was trying to blow us over the railing."

The anonymous writer had to thaw the lock before the door would open.

Although this cabin is on the national historic lookout register, accommodations are not as primitive as at most fire lookouts. The carpeted room has insulated windows, solar electric lights, cookware, a double bed with a comfy mattress, and a gas range complete with oven. The bathroom, admittedly, is a pit outhouse in a log structure accessible only by climbing down the stairs and crossing a snow drift.

At the lookout itself, the view's the thing. Even in storms, it's hard not to stare out the 16 windows as if at an IMAX surround-screen. Snowflakes blast the glass panes while streamers of fog rip through the frosted, wind-gnarled trees of the ridgecrest below.

Even when the wind roars like a jet engine the tower doesn't really shake or swing. It just creaks a bit. Salvaged from an abandoned lookout on Grass Mountain and reassembled here in 1985, the tower supporting the cabin is anchored on four sides by large cables. The cables are also part of a complicated system designed to divert lightning strikes.

When the clouds blow away, Diamond Peak looms directly to the east, a broad five-peaked snow fortress. To the south rise Mt. Thielsen's improbably sharp spire and Mt. Bailey's broad white hump. In the other direction, South Sister shines through a gap like a white beacon, with the tips of North and Middle Sister peeking out nearby.

Sunset ignites the mountains with pink. At night the windows turn black, save for a tiny constellation of lights from distant Oakridge and the flickering orange reflections of the propane stove's flame.

The Forest Service recommends carrying in all the water you will need. They cannot guarantee the purity of snow you might gather in the lookout's aluminum cookpots and melt over the propane woodstove. The Forest Service also asks that visitors use the outhouse at night rather than relieve themselves from the railing of the 41-foot tower. This is all sound advice, for many reasons.

Still, 10 miles is a long way to carry water. If you take your chances and melt snow to drink, be sure to gather it far enough away from the tower that it is absolutely, completely white.

Reservations are about $65 a night online at *www.recreation.gov*. Expect a $9-per-reservation service fee and a two-night minimum during weekends. Weekends are booked months in advance, but you can get a weekday reservation almost anytime.

Getting There: Drive a mile east of Oakridge on Highway 58 to a sign for Hills Creek Reservoir, turn right for half a mile to a junction, and turn right on Rigdon Road 21 for 17.4 paved miles. Then turn left on gravel Youngs Creek Road 2129 until you're stopped by snow—usually after three to five miles. If a snowstorm is coming you might park even sooner so your car won't get drifted in. Then ski or snowshoe up Road 2129. A mile beyond Moon Point's cliff, at the junction of spur Road 444, you face a decision. It's simplest to continue up Road 2129 for two miles and turn right on Road 439 for 4 miles to the lookout. But you can save 2 miles on a steeper, fainter ski trail if you turn right on spur Road 444 and shortcut through the woods past Moon Lake, following blue diamond markers to the lookout.

50

SKIING STEENS MOUNTAIN

Steens Mountain's East Rim in winter.

Why don't hordes of cross-country skiers flock to the glorious powder slopes on this stunning desert mountain range?

Let me count the reasons. First, Steens Mountain is a six-hour drive from the Willamette Valley—more than an hour beyond the remote town of Burns, Oregon. Second, skiing to the summit demands an uphill climb of some 4000 feet in about 14 miles, so you need at least three days. Third, the area's volatile weather can bring howling windstorms, whiteouts, and subzero temperatures at a moment's notice.

Despite these difficulties—or perhaps because of them—skiing to the top of Steens Mountain remains one of the greatest backcountry adventures in the lower 48 states. Where else can you ski a 6-mile downhill run, entirely above timberline, through mind-boggling Antarctic scenery?

The first step in planning the trip is to get the required, free Steens winter recreation permit by calling the Bureau of Land Management in Burns at (541) 573-4400. The permit lets you pick up a key to the locked gate at the base of the mountain, saving you a day's march up the road to the actual beginning of snow. The permit has another advantage, too. Once the BLM issues a skiing permit, they close the mountain to snowmobiles for that date, so you'll have the place to yourself.

Next head for Frenchglen, a windswept hamlet of about 30 that's an hour's drive south of Burns on paved Highway 205. The Frenchglen Hotel is a good place to steel yourself for the trek ahead.

In the morning it's a 2-mile drive on gravel to the Steens Mountain Road's locked gate. Snow levels vary a lot on the mountain, but we were able to drive 7 miles past the gate to the road's 6000-foot level. At that point, the lowlands' sparse, dotted juniper trees had just about given up, leaving only sagebrush and groves of wind-gnarled, white-barked quaking aspen.

A good goal for the first day of skiing is Fish Lake, a frozen pool another 6 miles up the road. There's a summer campground here, but in winter the picnic tabletops lie nearly flush with the windswept snowpack.

For the final 8 miles beyond Fish Lake, the roadbed disappears altogether beneath vast, treeless snowfields. If a blizzard rolls through,

We skied as far as the Fish Lake Campground the first day, halfway to the summit.

Little Blitzen Gorge is one of five canyons scalloping the mountain's tilted plateau.

you'll need more than a compass to find your way back across this tundra. Bring a topographic map and a GPS device.

Paralleling the final part of the route are sinuous, 3000-foot-deep chasms. The glaciers are gone that carved these enormous U-shaped valleys into the mountain's tilted plateau during the last Ice Age.

Finally you'll reach the abrupt edge of the plateau. This breathtaking 50-mile-long cliff teeters more than a mile above the shimmering playa of the Alvord Desert beyond. From the East Rim Viewpoint you can see six states on a clear day, from Wyoming's Grand Tetons to California's Warner Mountains.

On the blue-sky day when my four-person expedition skittered to the icy lip of the summit, howling winds sank the wind-chill factor to 30 below zero.

At first it seemed a dangerously lifeless spot. I briefly removed my gloves to change a camera lens, and within seconds my fingers were numb. But then, while piling rocks on my camera bag to keep it from blowing off into the void, I noticed a strange orange spot. To my astonishment, the underside of one rock was crowded with thousands of ladybugs, massed together for warmth, patiently waiting for spring to return to the top of this 9,733-foot mountain.

Such proof of life's tenacity can warm the spirit better than a crackling campfire. Our group took in the cataclysmic rim's view one last time. Then we turned our skis for the trip back—and the thrill of Oregon's only 6-mile-long ski run above timberline.

Quaking aspen trees at Fish Lake.

JANUARY
IN OREGON

51

KINGS VALLEY: A STEP BACK IN TIME

Two parks northwest of Corvallis showcase the history and beauty of Kings Valley, a key center during Oregon's pioneer years. Here you can inspect the site of a Civil War-era Army fort, visit two pioneer homestead farmhouses, and stroll alongside a splashing mountain creek. For a quick tour, hike a short loop at each of the two parks. If you have more time, extend the loops by climbing forested hills to viewpoints.

As in the neighboring Willamette Valley, the Kalapuya tribe in Kings Valley traditionally used fire to manage the land, burning off grass and fir seedlings each year. The resulting oak savanna provided a wealth of food—edible camas flower bulbs, acorns, and tarweed seeds, as well as easily huntable deer.

Beginning in the 1770s, however, disastrous plagues of smallpox and other "white man's" diseases killed up to 95 percent of the native people.

When Nahum King led a group of 25 Oregon Trail pioneers to stake out

Left: Crater Lake's Phantom Ship in winter.   Above: In Kings Valley, a 1930s barn has been renovated as a learning center at the Beazell Memorial Forest.

farms in Kings Valley in 1846, the decimated tribe offered no resistance. Nonetheless, the Army rounded up Indians from all of western Oregon onto a reservation that encompassed the northern Coast Range. Then the military secured the reservation borders with three outposts.

Today Fort Hoskins seems an unlikely location for an Army base. When it opened in 1856, however, it stood at the intersection of two major Indian trails.

The Frantz-Dunn house at Fort Hoskins.

The fort changed its focus during the Civil War, keeping an eye on settlers sympathetic to the Confederacy. When the war ended in 1865, the Army abandoned the fort. The site was sold to a family that lived and farmed there until 1992.

Meanwhile, a different pioneer family settled 3 miles away on the other side of the Luckiamute River. Ashnah Plunkett, the first white child born in Kings Valley, had met her husband at a local dance. He was a California soldier serving as a drummer at Fort Hoskins. Together they built a white clapboard farmhouse along Plunkett Creek in 1875. Ashnah lived there until her death in 1933.

By the 1960s, the area's economy was shifting from farming to forestry.

The Plunkett Creek Loop tours a mossy canyon at the Beazell Memorial Forest.

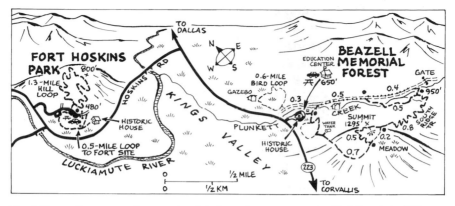

Fred Beazell, an employee at a high-tech company in California's Silicon Valley, bought the Plunkett farm as a vacation retreat in 1966. He started planting trees there in his spare time. Fred married his long-time sweetheart Dolores in 1968 and finally convinced her to move to Oregon in 1991.

But Dolores Beazell died just two years later. Grieving, and without children, Fred decided to leave the 586-acre property to the public in

Getting To Beazell Memorial Forest: From Corvallis, drive west on Highway 20 toward the Coast 10 miles. Turn north at a big sign for Kings Valley between mileposts 46 and 45. Follow Highway 223 for 4.8 miles to a sign for the Beazell Memorial Forest and turn right to a gravel parking turnaround. At both parks, dogs must be on leash or under voice control.

Hiking Tips: Cross a picnic lawn, continue straight past a barn, veer left across a footbridge, and turn right on an old roadbed. After half a mile following Plunkett Creek, fork to the right on the Plunkett Creek Loop, a smaller graveled path closer to the creek. After another half mile—and just 100 feet beyond a high, 60-foot railed footbridge—watch closely for an easy-to-miss junction with the South Ridge Trail on the right. (If you cross a second high footbridge, you've gone 100 feet too far.)

At this junction you face a decision. For a short hike, simply continue straight 200 feet on the Plunkett Creek Loop and turn left on an old roadbed back down to your car. For a more vigorous hike, turn right on the South Ridge Trail. This longer route climbs in 20 switchbacks to a big junction with a mapboard. If you turn right here and keep right at junctions you'll climb 0.2 mile to a forested hilltop, zigzag down 0.3 mile beside a meadow, and follow an old roadbed 0.7 mile back to your car.

Getting to Fort Hoskins: From the Beazell Memorial Forest, drive a few hundred yards back to Highway 223, turn right (north) for 1.7 miles to milepost 25, turn left on Hoskins Road for 1.8 miles, and turn right on the park's steep entrance road for 0.4 mile to a paved parking area, where the road is gated closed.

memory of his beloved wife. Today Benton County manages the land to provide hiking trails and restore forest ecology. Logging is permitted only to pay the park's expenses.

Start your visit at the Beazell Memorial Forest. The Plunketts' original farmhouse still stands in the middle of the parking loop. For the hike, cross a picnic lawn to the Plunketts' 1930s barn, now tastefully modernized as a learning center. Then follow Plunkett Creek upstream as far as you like.

For your next stop in Kings Valley, head for Fort Hoskins Historical Park. At the parking area here, a picnic shelter in an old apple orchard here looks out across the fort site to the distant Luckiamute River and a few scattered farmhouses — all that remains of the town of Hoskins.

For a half-mile tour of the fort site, walk down the gated road 200 yards and turn right on a wide gravel path. Just beyond a sign describing the fort's parade grounds, detour briefly left down a road to the Frantz-Dunn House, built in 1869 by the family that bought the fort. Then continue on the gravel loop trail back up to the picnic area.

For a longer hike, look for a small trail sign opposite the restrooms at the start of the paved parking area. Take this path up through Douglas fir woods 200 yards and fork to the right.

The 1.3-mile loop that begins here switchbacks up a hill through a restored oak savanna. Park managers have cut invasive firs to release the old oaks favored by the Kalapuyans' ancient system of fire management.

The top of Fort Hoskins' restored meadow has a view across the head of Kings Valley, but if you know the story here, it's really a view across Oregon's history.

A walking tour of the site of Civil War-era Fort Hoskins begins at a picnic shelter.

52

Skiing Around Three Fingered Jack

Our campsite at First Creek Meadow.

Overnight trips in the winter wilderness are inherently dangerous. What left me feeling closest to mortality, however, was the time I skied around Three Fingered Jack and found an airplane that had recently crashed in the snow.

Together with a cadre of ski chums, I had planned to ski with 50-pound backpacks from Santiam Pass to the base of Three Fingered Jack, deep in the Mount Jefferson Wilderness. There we would set up a base camp in First Creek Meadow and spend the next day skiing around the mountain.

Five days before our trip a small Cessna airplane smacked into the shoulder of Three Fingered Jack. The three people on board died instantly. In their twenties, they had been on a sightseeing tour of an area burned

by a forest fire. National Guards-
men with a Blackhawk helicopter
managed to retrieve the bodies
three days after the crash. But
they left the plane.

As we were skiing the five
rugged, trailless miles through
black snags toward the base of
Three Fingered Jack, I noticed a
flash of silver in the sky. It was
a commercial jet, perhaps on its
way to Portland or Seattle.

Suddenly I remembered the
many times I had trekked into
the wilderness, trying to leave the

A difficult traverse to the Pacific Crest Trail.

cares of civilization behind, only
to have the distant roar of aircraft engines cut into my solitude. More than
once I had photographed a lonely mountain, only to notice later that the
picture was marred by a white contrail of ice crystals in the stratosphere.

Of course I know the other side of that equation—I know how strange
it is to be eating peanuts nervously in a narrow seat while white speck-
led forests slip by far below an ovoid plastic window. When you are

*Five days earlier, three people had died in a
plane crash on Three Fingered Jack.*

30,000 feet in the air, it's hard to
imagine what life could possibly
be like down there in the snowy
wilderness. These are worlds that
should never meet, universes of
matter and antimatter.

The closer we skied to the
mountain, the more green trees
we saw. The wildfire that swept
through the southern half of the
Mt. Jefferson Wilderness in 2003
had petered out in the canyons
near timberline. Rock cliffs and
gaps in the forest had stopped the
flames.

In the last grove of gnarled mountain hemlocks before Three Fingered
Jack's gigantic east face, we tramped circles into the snow to create flat
spots to pitch our tents. We lit our backpacking stoves to melt drinking
water and cook dinner. Then the stars came out, the temperature dropped

OREGON FAVORITES

below freezing, and we crawled into our thick down sleeping bags.

The next morning dawned so sunny and warm that we set off around the mountain skiing in our undershirts. By noon we chanced upon the wreck, just above the Pacific Crest Trail, high on the mountain's southwest flank. If the plane had been 280 feet higher, it would have cleared a pass and sailed safely back to Bend.

Telemark turns at Canyon Creek Meadows.

The small airplane's tail was almost intact, but both wings lay detached beside the fuselage, as if discarded there. The engine and propeller were buried beneath the snow. Shards of blue Plexiglas windowpanes littered the slope. The seats had been twisted backwards inside a crumpled shell of bent metal. The plane's skin seemed as thin as a soda pop can.

Lying in the snow was a baseball visor. Two headphones, one with its cord ripped asunder. A headrest.

This was a solemn site, where dimensions had collapsed into chaos.

From the Pacific Crest Trail, Mt. Washington towers to the south.

All day long a procession of small planes droned past the mountain, tipping their wings as they banked for a look. It was the first Saturday since the crash, but I could sense these fliers were not here as voyeurs, out of morbid curiosity. They were here to pay their respects.

I imagined that each pilot was visualizing the final seconds, the decision to fly low through a notch by the summit, the surprising downdraft that swept over the Cascade crest, the unusual east wind.

"I don't think we should stay here any longer," one of my friends said quietly. Without a word we followed him on a long traverse across the snowy flank of Three Fingered Jack. We did not speak again for a full mile,

At a cornice we looked down a 800-foot drop into Canyon Creek Meadows.

until we reached a stand of big mountain hemlock trees that had survived the fire.

For the rest of the day we continued onward around the mountain, clockwise, cresting a dozen ridges and a dozen silent, snowy valleys. The view shifted slowly and grandly, from the Three Sisters to Mount Washington's spire, to Hoodoo's bald head, to Coffin Mountain's gigantic stone bier, to half-frozen Marion Lake, to the huge white teepee of Mount Jefferson.

In the afternoon we reached the biggest obstacle to any circumnavigation of Three Fingered Jack. Canyon Creek Meadows is a giant glacial bowl 800 feet deep, scooped out of the mountain's west flank. This a

lovely place to hike in summer. In winter, skiing off the canyon rim felt like leaping out of an airplane with only skis to slow my fall. I linked 80 Telemark turns. At the bottom, exhausted, we put skins on our skis so we could climb out the other side of the canyon to our camp.

I will admit that one of the reasons we undertake this kind of backcountry winter challenge is to prove we are still alive. Without risk, there is no adventure. Without exploring the edges of life, how can one know where the center lies?

My ski group, and the light planes, were circling Three Fingered Jack that weekend to find ourselves.

The 11-year-old son of one of my ski chums has sewn us a set of hats emblazoned with the logo "GST." He says it stands for "Geezer Ski Team."

We'll be wearing the hats proudly. We may be over fifty, but we're still alive, and we're not yet over every hill.

FEBRUARY
IN OREGON

A mural in The Dalles depicts Celilo Falls.

53

THE SHADOW OF CELILO FALLS

The Dalles Dam silenced the thunder of Celilo Falls in 1957, but the magic of that Columbia River spiritual center still echoes. This is particularly true at Columbia Hills, a Washington state park where you'll find salvaged petroglyphs, trails, a rock climbing area, and a historic ranch.

Start your voyage in The Dalles, a once-sleepy burg that woke up fast when Google opened offices here. Dozens of historic murals splash the old brick walls of new espresso cafes and kiteboard shops.

Before crossing the Columbia River, pause at the Oregon end of The Dalles Bridge. Water roars from the spillways of the dam that drowned Celilo Falls. A few rickety fishing platforms and unpainted shacks recall the Indian salmon-fishing metropolis that once was the Northwest's economic hub.

Petroglyph Canyon lies two miles upstream—and a hundred feet underwater. Thousands of painted images of owls, mountain goats, lizards, hunters, and demons once made that 10-acre basalt gorge the richest rock art site in the Northwest.

The Dalles Dam drowned the falls in 1957.

Just before the dam's waters rose, the Army Corps of Engineers chiseled a few dozen of those petroglyphs loose. The artworks languished in storage until 1974, and then were exhibited under a fish ladder at the dam.

Tribal groups from the Nez Perce to Warm Springs objected that an important spiritual center had been violated. They complained that the artworks were displayed as if they were trophies from a vanquished foe.

In 2003 the petroglyphs returned to a site with dignity—the Temani Pesh-wa ("Written on Rock") Trail, not far from their original location. The paved walkway along a basalt rim is only 100 yards long. Guard cables and surveillance cameras protect the rock art from those who might be tempted to touch. The most impressive of the local petroglyphs, a table-sized goddess face called "She Who Watches," is out of sight around a corner, visitable only on tours guided by rangers.

If wind announces spirits, then this is the right place for such art. Gale-force winds blast the rock badlands almost constantly. The nearby

Petroglyphs rescued from the rising water are displayed at the Temani Pesh-wa Trail.

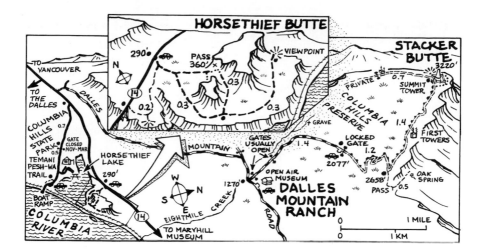

campground has plank fences beside each site to help keep tents from blowing away.

For a more substantial hike — and a chance to see the petroglpyhs' original home — drive a mile to the Horsethief Butte Trail. The butte is a mesa

Getting There: Take The Dalles Bridge north across the Columbia River, continue 3 miles, turn right on Washington Highway 14 for 1.6 miles, and then turn right for 1.8 miles through Columbia Hills State Park (formerly Horsethief Lake State Park) to a big gravel parking area on the left. A 100-yard paved walkway tours the petroglyphs, lined up along a basalt rim.

To Hike Horsethief Butte: Drive back to Highway 14 and turn east for 1.2 miles to a sign on the right for the Horsethief Butte Trail. Parking is tight on the shoulder near the sign. Dogs must be on leash. The hiking trail forks twice in the first 150 yards. Go left and then right. The path ends after 0.6 mile at a river viewpoint. The final 50 feet of the trail are crowded with poison oak, so long pants are best. After taking in the view, turn back for 0.3 mile to a trail junction. If you don't mind a little scrambling, turn uphill to the right on an alternate return route that climbs up a canyon and past a petroglyph.

To Visit the Dalles Mountain Ranch: Take Highway 14 back toward The Dalles 1.8 miles. Between mileposts 84 and 85, turn north on Dalles Mountain Road. Ignore a paved left-hand spur toward a winery and keep right on a wide, bumpy gravel road. After 2.5 miles you'll reach a fork. The hiking route is up to the left, but first turn right for 100 yards to tour the ranch headquarters. Then continue driving up the road 1.4 miles to a small parking area beside a locked gate. This final stretch of road is rough and passes two gates that can be closed. From the final gate (which is always locked), hike on up the road 2.6 miles to the summit of Stacker Butte.

A trail on Highway 14 has a view of Mt. Hood and one undisturbed petroglyph.

of columnar basalt that's popular with beginning rock climbers and casual hikers. The trail curves around the butte's base. Big yellow balsamroot flowers bloom among the sagebrush here in April. The path ends after 0.6 mile at a panoramic cliff overlooking the Columbia River.

If you want, you can simply return as you came. But if you don't mind a little scrambling, hike back 0.3 mile to a junction and turn uphill to the right through a miniature version of Petroglyph Canyon. The original basalt gorge is not far away, downhill to the south, now drowned by the reservoir. Near the summit of the trail across Horsethief Butte, a small warning sign alerts hikers (and climbers) to the faint red markings of one

Horsethief Butte overlooks the reservoir where Petroglyph Canyon lies.

The Dalles Mountain Ranch includes an outdoor museum of farm machinery.

petroglyph that has not been moved.

If you continue past the petroglyph, you'll need to use your hands to scramble over a rocky pass to return to your car.

What's next? Why not visit a historic ranch and hike to a much higher viewpoint nearby?

For this trip, drive a few miles up to the Dalles Mountain Ranch. Park by a weathered barn and walk 100 feet to the porch of a locked farmhouse. Then amble around the fields above the barn to see an exhibit of farm machinery — tillers, planters, balers, and graders near a pioneer cemetery.

The ranch dates to the late 1800s. Much of the relatively fertile soil on the rounded hills arrived as ash from Cascade Range volcanoes. Lower areas, including the angular scablands near Horsethief Butte, were stripped of soil by giant Ice Age floods that roared down the Columbia River from a glacial dam in northern Idaho 15,300 to 12,700 years ago.

The house at The Dalles Mountain Ranch.

For an overview of the entire region, continue driving up the ranch road to a locked gate. Then park and walk 2.6 miles up the old road to a spectacular view at the summit of 3220-foot Stacker Butte. Along the way you'll pass a first set of fairly ordinary radio towers. The summit, however, has an eerily fenced array with an air control wigwam.

The panorama here adds Mt. Adams to views of Mt. Hood and the great, snaking Columbia River.

If the spirits of Celilo have survived, they might well be howling here, high above the dam that flooded Celilo Falls and Petroglyph Canyon.

54

WITH OPB ON BROKEN TOP

At first I didn't believe that Ed Jahn could be a producer for the most popular television show filmed in Oregon. He seemed too young.

A soft-spoken man in his 20s, with spectacles and a blond goatee, Ed approached me after I'd given a slide show about one of my hiking guidebooks at Powell's Bookstore in Portland. He was enthused about something I mentioned in my slide show—that I've been tackling Oregon backcountry ski adventures with several Eugene chums.

Ed wanted to join us on our next adventure—an attempt to ski around Broken Top, a route that is trailless even in summer.

But then he said his camera crew would need to bring along 400 pounds of gear. That seemed an impossible obstacle. Skiers could never carry that much weight. I took Ed's card, but shook my head.

Months later, after I'd given a slide show at the Sunriver library, I was approached by a different soft-spoken young man, Rodney "Bino" Fowler. An amateur dog sled racer, he offered to take me with him on a trip someday.

"How much weight can your dogs pull?" I wondered aloud.

"About 400 pounds," Bino replied.

Bingo! I notified Ed and my ski chums that the trip was possible

A dozen huskies pulled television equipment to Broken Top's crater. Opposite: Tam McArthur Rim, one of the trip's obstacles.

after all. The sled dogs would haul the camera crew's gear nine miles to a wilderness base camp at an elevation of 8020 feet in the crater of Broken Top. From there we four skiers could attempt the 11-mile, largely trailless circuit of the peak carrying digital video cameras.

And so we all rendezvoused at the Dutchman Flat Sno-Park near Mt. Bachelor at 8am on a wintry Friday morning. Everyone was nervous because the sky was overcast with an approaching storm.

The camera crew included three of OPB's youngest, most energetic people. Ed, 29, would be in charge of interviews. The cameraman, Nick Fisher, in his 30s, had worked at KVAL-TV in Eugene from 1994 to 1997 before signing on with Oregon Field Guide. Owen Wosniak, 26, was the crew's gofer, assigned to set up tents and lug camera tripods.

I learned later that Owen is a Harvard graduate and a Rhodes Scholar interning at Oregon Field Guide for experience. He volunteered for this trip, hoping to get in a little snowboarding.

The twelve Siberian huskies were on hand, already yipping and tugging at their anchored sled.

Ed surprised us by marshaling some backup transportation—two snowmobiles and a gigantic $200,000 Bombardier snow-grooming tractor, driven by volunteers from the local snowmobile club. These machines could go with us the first six miles, but would have to turn back at the Three Sisters Wilderness Area boundary.

Never had my group of backcountry skiers set out on a trip with such an entourage. In the lead lurched the tractor, grooming a tidy 12-foot-wide path. Close behind raced the dogs, yelping and straining with their sled. Then came the two snowmobiles, zooming ahead to set up the camera every few miles to film us as we slowly skied past with our backpacks.

At the Wilderness boundary the clouds lowered, plunging the treeless slopes ahead into a whiteout. The snow machines turned back. Owen went ahead with Bino and the dogsled to find the little frozen lake I'd chosen as our campsite—no easy task with visibility at 100 feet. I gave Owen my global positioning device and wished him luck.

We skiers followed the dog tracks, slowed now by Ed and Nick, who trudged on snowshoes and stopped often to film.

After an hour of slow progress Ed used a walkie-talkie to call ahead to Owen. Yes, he had found the frozen lake, or at least *a* frozen lake, in the whiteout. But Bino and the dogs had already headed for home.

Owen was alone, huddled on a pile of gear in gale-force winds. He added, "I hope you get here soon."

When we reached the crater campsite Nick set the television camera on time-lapse. I imagine it will appear that our tents pop up like magic. Then speed-shovelers will sculpt the snow into windbreaks and benches.

We crawled into our thick down sleeping bags at 7:30pm, but I couldn't sleep for hours. Forty-mile-an-hour gusts shook the tent all night with the violence of a deranged yeti.

Ed Jahn and his camera crew at 8020 feet.

I wearily unzipped the tent flap at 6:30am and was astonished to find the colossal crags of Broken Top looming directly in front of us, bathed in sunshine. A gap in the storm had given us blue sky and a chance at our goal.

The camera crew began frantically filming. They were upset that they had slept through the chance to get a time-lapse shot of the sunrise.

I had planned our circuit of

Dawn brought blue sky and hope to our camp atop Broken Top's cirque lake.

Broken Top to begin with the most dangerous slope: the thousand-foot drop off of Tam McArthur Rim. Now I could see that the pass I'd chosen near Broken Hand consisted of bare rock. It did not look good.

However, a faint set of old ski tracks led to a higher, snowier pass on the shoulder of Broken Top itself. The seven of us—skiers and camera crew—climbed to this new, high pass without knowing what we'd find on the far side.

The pass provided a breathtaking, close-up view of all Three Sisters. To the left and right stood sheer rock cliffs capped with curling, 20-foot ice cornices. Directly ahead lay a not-impossibly-steep slope of glare ice beside the Bend Glacier.

With the cameras rolling, the four of us skied off one at a time, skis clattering and slipping on the ice. Talbot Bielefeldt, a former ski instructor, managed to make a few impressive turns. I suspect the rest of us did not look so graceful.

Talbot Bielefeldt pauses on the trailless 11-mile trek around Broken Top.

Then the television crew returned to camp for the day. We four skiers sallied onward around the mountain.

The ice softened to corn snow as we skied down into the beautiful Green Lakes Basin. A bank of clouds boiled behind South Sister, cooking up an odd blizzard that left us in a snowstorm under a sunny blue sky.

By afternoon the snow was so slushy that our skis set off a small slide. With this warning, we spread out and turned on our avalanche beacons. The radio transmitters strapped to our chests would help us locate each other if one of us was buried in snow.

As the day waned and our energy ebbed, we attached climbing skins to the bottoms of our skis to gain traction for the arduous climb back up to camp.

The television crew, rested and ready, met us at the tents with cameras rolling. "Now let's see you break out the whisky and toast your victory," Ed said.

I looked at him and shook my head. "I hope that's not how you plan to end this film."

"Why not?"

"Because we didn't conquer Broken Top. Coming out here isn't about conquering things."

Alan MCullough backed me up. "He's right. A trip like this is about teamwork."

OREGON FAVORITES

"And adventure," Talbot added.

Tony Diehl said, "It may sound corny, but it's like getting closer to God."

Ed exchanged glances with the cameraman. "All right. There's lots of ways we could end this. We'll see what works."

That evening, with the television camera set up above camp, we put our flashlights into Talbot's orange tent, lighting it like a full moon rising from the dark camp. Alan stood silhouetted beside the tent with the bamboo flute he'd brought, improvising a haunting melody that echoed across the crater. Untwinkling stars marked the dark crags of Broken Top overhead.

To me, the scene captured the wild spirit and the solitude I seek on backcountry ski expeditions.

"The starlight shot was nice," Ed admitted the next morning as we were packing up. "But I'm not sure it will match the sunrise time-lapse."

"Sunrise? I thought you forgot to turn on your camera for that."

"The first night we forgot. But this morning we remembered."

"But—" I now recalled seeing the camera, on a tripod facing our tents. "But the first thing the four of us did this morning was go outside and, well, you know. Yellow snow."

Ed grinned. "Imagine that speeded up in time lapse."

He left me curious to see how the youngest and most daring producer at Oregon Field Guide would would end the television episode.

The Green Lakes at South Sister, a crowded destination in summer, are silent in winter.

FARTHER
AFIELD

A laska on $12 a day!

At least that was my goal in the summer of 1995, when I set out to plan a family trip to the Last Frontier. I was feeling cocky after having taken my wife, 15-year-old daughter, and 13-year-old son camping across Oregon the previous year at the same low-budget rate.

Then I found out it costs $12 a day just to park a car at the Seattle airport. From there we'd have to swim.

While scrambling for alternatives I discovered the Alaska Marine Highway.

This state-owned ferry system lets you cruise the scenic island-dotted Inside Passage from Bellingham, Washington to Juneau on the cheap. The trick is to leave the car behind and sail as a foot passenger. The half dozen ferries that service the Southeast Alaska panhandle share the route with

humpback whales, orcas, bald eagles, and occasional small blue icebergs from tidewater glaciers.

If you steam straight through in two days and two nights the basic adult fare from Bellingham to Juneau is just a couple of hundred dollars. Even if you stop for layovers at four towns along the way (a six-day trip at least), the price is the same—far less than the commercial cruises based in Vancouver, Canada.

Yes, but where do you sleep? Ferry cabins are such a bargain that they're often booked six months in advance,

Alaska state ferries sail the Inside Passage from Bellingham (above).

Budget ferry travelers camp on the deck.   Below: Sitka was Alaska's Russian capital.

especially on the Bellingham-Ketchikan run. The ferry office sells twice as many passenger tickets as there are berths. Their booklet suggests that passengers without berths bring sleeping bags. And, perhaps, a tent.

A tent?

So we showed up at the Bellingham terminal with sleeping bags and a tent in our bulging backpacks. When the gate opened, hundreds of similarly laden travelers dashed aboard to claim the best tent sites on the decks open to camping.

Of course you can't pound a tent stake into a ship's steel deck. Wiser travelers had brought duct tape. We borrowed a roll to secure the edges and wedged our tent in a tight spot near the railing. By then the deck had bloomed with a colorful crop of nylon domes, like a box jam-packed with balloons.

At first the romance of tenting on deck was intoxicating. But the ferry travels at 20 miles per hour, so there's a stiff breeze even in fine weather. That night an additional headwind created a gale. Five tents blew flat at 2am amid shouts of alarm. One party fled indoors to the observation lounge, where sleeping bags are allowed on the carpet at night. Their abandoned tent promptly sailed over the railing, carrying the rest of their gear to sea. In the morning we folded our tent and moved indoors for the duration.

Each ferry includes a cafeteria, a restaurant, a bar, a solarium, and inexpensive showering facilities. Often, an on-board Forest Service guide gives talks and points out sights.

As cruise ships go, the ferries are humble, but the camaraderie on board is infectious. You rub shoulders with genuine Alaskans: Tlingit grandmothers with beadwork necklaces, cannery workers headed for grueling summer jobs, and high school athletes traveling to away games on neighboring islands.

Hotels are expensive and crowded in Alaska, so I plotted our itinerary to avoid them altogether. Each day we'd go ashore to see a town, and each evening we'd hop an overnight ferry to the next village.

First stop was Ketchikan, Alaska's southernmost and rainiest city. On a huge island sheltering the seldom seen Misty Fiords National Monument Wilderness, Ketchikan is best known for its totem pole museums. Also don't

Even in mid-summer, muskeg and muddy trails mean hikers need rubber boots.

miss Creek Street, a former red-light district perched on boardwalks above a stream full of thrashing salmon. The old bordellos have been yuppified into art boutiques and espresso delis.

Next stop for us was Petersburg, a fishing village founded by Norwegians. The Sons of Norway lodge is the town's second largest building— after the new supermarket, where the aisles are labeled in both English and Norwegian.

Petersburg is surrounded by muskeg, a weird bogscape covered with such a thick layer of floating sphagnum moss that small pine trees can grow atop it, entirely afloat. Fifteen percent of Southeast Alaska is muskeg. Hiking trails in this terrain are planked for miles so you don't sink through.

Sitka, the old Russian capital of Alaska, lies a ten-hour ferry trip north of Petersburg. The onion-domed Russian Orthodox cathedral and its bishop's residence remain from the 1840s.

We set aside most of our time, however, to explore Juneau, Alaska's current capital.

We rented a car there. This may seem strange if you know that Juneau has hardly 100 miles of roads. The city is cut off from the rest of the world by glaciers descending from a Rhode-Island-sized ice cap.

My strategy was that a car would save on taxi fares to the city's famous museums and hiking trails. A car would also get us to the inexpensive and fabulously scenic Forest Service campground at the foot of the colossal Mendenhall Glacier, just past the Fred Meyer shopping center in Juneau's suburbs.

The man at Rent-A-Wreck politely loaded our baggage into a flawless-looking Ford and sent us off with a big smile. This prevented us from immediately discovering that the hatchback tended to snap shut like a guillotine during loading.

I gradually learned to accept that the vehicle had no emergency brake, horn, or turn signals. But when the engine suddenly died on Juneau's only freeway, I walked back to the rental office to complain.

The smiling man said, "Died, eh? And the ignition whines?"

"That's right!" I exclaimed.

"Happens all the time. Here, try another."

Before I drove off again I asked, "Where do you get these cars?"

He shrugged. "Eugene."

"Eugene! As in Oregon?" My hometown, 1200 miles away, seemed an unlikely source.

He explained that Alaskan drivers are so reckless and the roads so bad that he won't buy used cars for his rental company there. Likewise, traffic in Seattle and Portland leaves most cars there dinged. So twice a year he buys a load of shiny used cars at a Eugene auction, trucks them to Seattle, and barges them to Juneau. On average, they last a year.

We began to worry about the campground, too. The local paper had reported that police were searching for a senseless vandal who had wrecked several campsites without stealing anything of value.

We spotted the culprit right away. He was sitting on a picnic table, licking jam out of a jar. Harry, as we came to call this wayward black bear, eventually became the target of an interagency keystone cops chase involving weenies, chicken wings, and tranquilizer darts.

More puzzling than the vandal mystery was the sign at the campground entrance: "Absolutely No Forklift Pallets." None of the campers seemed to have a forklift. Why should they?

But then one night at 1am, in the midst of a torrential downpour, two pickup trucks squealed into the empty campsite next to ours. A half dozen young people piled out, unloaded several forklift pallets, chopped them up with an ax, and built a huge bonfire. After an hour of raucous drinking they smashed their liquor bottles into the fire and drove off.

In the morning I was surveying the charred debris when the campground host walked up. He shook his head grimly. "Forklift pallets, eh?"

Apparently firewood is scarce in Juneau, but pallets are plentiful because nearly all supplies arrive by ship. Even campground signs can't keep rowdy summer workers from burning them at drinking parties.

Our coziest night in Juneau was spent near a woodstove in a candlelit log cabin deep in the wilderness. The Forest Service maintains nearly a hundred of these rustic cabins in Southeast Alaska. The rent is nominal, even by Oregon standards. Most are accessible only by float plane or sea kayak. But several are on the excellent hiking trail network fringing Juneau.

The Alaska state ferries service such a vast area that a three-week trip can only sample it. We did not, for example, sail as far as Skagway, the Gold Rush boomtown that survives as a tourist trap. Nor did we venture onto the wilder ferry routes that range from Valdez and Kodiak to the far-flung Aleutian Islands.

And of course, $12 a day proved to be an unrealistic budget for Alaska. But sailing the state ferries of the beautiful Inside Passage is surely one of the most economical and fun ways to explore the Last Frontier.

At Juneau, the Mendenhall Glacier (below) launches icebergs into a lake (opposite).

56

A Birthday in Victoria

Janell poses by totem poles in Victoria on a surprise birthday trip.

My wife Janell worried about her fiftieth birthday. "It's not something I want friends and family to celebrate," she admitted a month before the date.

I nodded. Half a century is a delicate age. "The only safe way to avoid a surprise party is to leave town."

"Leave town?"

"You know, take a trip. Ideally, we'd leave the country altogether for a week."

"What a great idea!"

"Good. I'll plan the whole thing."

She beamed for a minute. Then she asked, "But where would we go?"

"This trip is my present to you, and presents are usually secret."

"You'd choose someplace nice?"

"Of course."

"OK. Let it be a surprise."

We said no more about it for a while. But curiosity began to get the better of her. Three weeks before her birthday she asked, "Have you had any luck planning my birthday trip?"

"It's all set. You wanted it to be a surprise, remember?"

"At least give me a clue."

"It involves an island."

For the next week I heard her musing about Hawaii, the Caribbean, and Ireland.

Amtrak trains roll to Seattle in style.

Then she confronted me again. "How can I pack if I don't know where we're going? Should I take an umbrella or a swimsuit? Do we need our passports?"

"Passports would be a good idea. And you might need both the umbrella and the swimsuit. But pack light. We're not allowed to take more than 35 pounds of luggage."

"Oh!" Her voice betrayed a bit of alarm. Neither Hawaii nor Ireland would limit luggage that much. What kind of island had I booked?

She held out until five days before our scheduled departure. Then she broke down and begged to know where we were going.

I told her I had planned to have a stretch limousine pick us up, drive us toward the airport, make a feint toward the coast, and then swing back downtown to the train station. That ruse was no longer necessary.

We were going to Vancouver Island.

This is actually an extremely fun trip if you leave the car at home. The

The Victoria Clipper, a hydrofoil, zooms out of Seattle on a two-hour cruise to an island.

trick is to start by taking Amtrak to Seattle. You get on the train in Oregon in the morning and ride the rails north along the Columbia River and Puget Sound. Riverscapes with herons and bald eagles roll past your picture windows. Grab a meal on board or bring your own picnic. If it's foggy, watch the movie they show along the way.

When you reach Seattle in the afternoon, you'll be glad if you've packed your luggage in a backpack. Then you can walk a mile north through Old Town to Pike Place Market. Just beyond the market is Pier 69, where the fast ferry to Victoria departs.

This high-speed hydrofoil makes the journey to Canada in two hours. The Seattle sklyine with the Space Needle shrinks into the wake as you zoom away.

The hydrofoil docks in the heart of Victoria's harbor, where Hudson's Bay traders set up shop 200 years ago. If you've planned ahead as I did, you've booked a room in a bed & breakfast within walking distance of the bay. Our inn had a funky suite in the attic of an old garden house with views across the city. Breakfast was substantial and British, with bangers and fried tomatoes.

Tourist buses leave Victoria each morning for Butchart Gardens, the limestone quarry converted to a tourist attraction by a bored cement manufacturer's wife. We shunned this pleasant tourist trap for the fabulous Royal BC Museum in downtown Victoria and the less well-known hiking trails nearby.

One of the hiking highlights is Mystic Beach, where a waterfall pours

into the ocean beside a cave. The path to the hidden beach is part of a trail system that traces the southwest shore of Vancouver Island more than 100 miles from Victoria to Barkley Sound.

Our loft in a Victoria bed & breakfast inn.

The trail system consists of three very different sections: The Galloping Goose Trail, the Juan de Fuca Trail, and the West Coast Trail. The routes becomes progressively wilder, the farther west you explore from Victoria.

The Galloping Goose Trail

The "Goose", as it's known to locals, is a paved bike path that follows an abandoned railroad grade 29 miles west from downtown Victoria to the coastal village of Sooke. The trail's name honors a railway car that carried passengers on this logging railroad route in the 1920s.

The path begins at the Johnston Street Bridge in Victoria's harbor. The paved trail here is popular with bicycle commuters and in-line skaters. After a mile the trail recrosses Victoria's harbor on a 1000-foot wooden trestle and sets off through the suburbs. Eventually the nearly level route traverses forested parks with ocean views.

At Sooke, the Goose turns inland for 5 miles to its end at Leechtown, a gold mining camp dating to 1868. To continue along the shore, you'll need to bike or drive 15 miles west from Sooke along rustic Highway 14 to China Beach, the trailhead for a wilder, unpaved section of the coastal trail route.

The Juan de Fuca Trail

Completed in 1994, this rugged 29-mile hiking path climbs through wilderness rainforest from one remote beach to the next, tracing the shore of Vancouver Island between China Beach near River Jordan to Botanical Beach near Port Refrew.

Views extend across the Strait

A cave at Mystic Beach has a view across the Juan de Fuca Strait to Washington.

of Juan de Fuca to the white-capped Olympic Mountains of Washington State.

Because Highway 14 meets the trail at four points along the way, it's easy to break the trip up into day hikes. A daily van service, the West Coast Trail Express, shuttles hikers between trailheads or back to Victoria.

Advance permits are not required to hike the Juan de Fuca Trail, but expect a $5-per-car parking fee at trailheads, and an additional $5-per-night fee if you're backpacking. Tenting is allowed only on beach sand.

By far the most popular parts of the Juan de Fuca Trail are its two ends. From the China Beach Trailhead at the east end of the route, a fun 3-mile trail segment leads down to Mystic Beach's cave and waterfall.

From the Botanical Beach Trailhead at the west end of the route, a 3-mile loop tours a rocky shoreline with tidepools.

Because Vancouver Island was covered by Ice Age glaciers just 6000 years ago, the forest soil is thinner and the trees are more gnarly than in Oregon. As a result the trails are rougher, with roots, bare rock, and mud-holes in wet weather. Good boots are essential.

The West Coast Trail

Beyond Port Refrew, Vancouver Island's Pacific shore becomes so rough that there are no roads. The 46-mile West Coast Trail along this coast began in the 1800s as an emergency escape route for shipwrecked sailors. The coast here has claimed more than 60 ships, including the Valencia in 1906, with the loss of 117 lives.

Today the West Coast Trail includes numerous ladders at cliffs, two private ferries at inlets, and five hand-operated cable cars across chasms. The trek takes five to seven days.

Water taxis connect downtown Vancouver with Granville Island's shops.

Open from May 1 to September 30, the route has become such a popular backpacking challenge that only 60 people a day are allowed to set out. Reservations cannot be made more than three months in advance, but it's also possible to show up at the trailhead without a reservation because unused permits are often available.

After three days of hiking and playing tourist on Vancouver Island for Janell's 50th birthday, we shouldered our backpacks and walked down to the harbor in Victoria.

"That was fun," Janell said, "But I think you misled me a little."

"What do you mean?"

"Well, we never really were limited to 35 pounds of luggage. And the trip wasn't quite a full week."

Float planes regularly make the 40-minute hop from Victoria to Vancouver (above).

"That's because your birthday trip isn't over yet."

"What?"

I walked past the ferry landing and kept going. She followed, puzzled. On the far side of the harbor I led her out a dock to a float plane. A man in a uniform took my tickets and checked that our luggage wasn't over-weight.

"Where on earth are you taking me?" Janell asked.

The plane was so small that I had to sit in the co-pilot's seat. The pilot suggested, during take-off, that I remove my foot from the footrest, because I was in fact depressing a rudder that steered us to the left.

With a terrific roar, the plane picked up speed across the harbor. The pontoons thudded repeatedly as they skipped along the tops of waves. Then we soared free, banked steeply over the strait, and headed east. For forty minutes we flew over a patchwork of islands. Then we swooped around the skyscrapers of Vancouver and splashed to stop in British Columbia's largest harbor.

The bed & breakfast I had chosen in Vancouver was less than a mile away, so we walked. Chinatown, Stanley Park, Granville Island — we explored the city for two days before catching a train back to the south.

Every birthday needs a little bit of surprise.

57

Spirits of Mount Shasta

Is Mount Shasta haunted, or just inspiring? This Northern California peak is held sacred by more than a dozen different religious groups. If one believes them all, the mountain must be crowded with deities.

I decided to visit Mount Shasta twice—once on a summer backpacking trip and once on a winter snow camping expedition—to see how the various resident spirits are getting along.

For the summer trip we headed out in August, drove south on Interstate 5, took the Central Mount Shasta exit, drove east through the city of Mount Shasta for a mile, and curved left onto the Everitt Memorial Highway—the only paved road that climbs to timberline.

The Everitt Memorial Highway deadends after 14 miles at a cluster of giant parking lots that remain from a vanished ski resort.

When developers originally built the Mount Shasta Ski Bowl Resort, members of the local Wintu tribe warned that the spirit of the mountain would be angry. The Wintu believe that Mount Shasta is the great white wigwam of a powerful god. Legends say the smoke that sometimes curls from the mountain's summit is the spirit's wigwam fire. To the Wintu, the entire area above timberline is sacred, and taboo.

One winter, after the ski resort had operated a few seasons, a massive avalanche roared down the mountain, obliterating all trace of the development. Buildings, pylons, and chairlifts were swept away, leaving only a lovely mountain meadow and a cluster of parking lots.

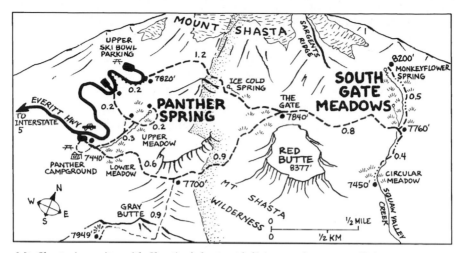

Mt. Shasta (opposite, with Shastina's butte at left) is sacred to many religious groups.

Today the Panther Meadow area at the lowest of the parking lots has a small, walk-in campground and a trailhead for paths leading into the Mount Shasta Wilderness.

Janell and I hefted our backpacks and set out on the trail. From the nearby campground we could hear chanting, drumming, and bits of conversation: "I went to the spring at dawn and could feel the wholeness." "How am I supposed to cook out here?" "I've heard there's a really spiritual place on Kauai too."

These campground people were evidently not Wintu. A Forest Service sign at the trailhead, beside the usual notices to "Leave No Trace," notes that the Wintu traditionally did not come here to drum, chant, or meditate. They did not come here at all.

But Mount Shasta's magnetism has been drawing visitors from other cultures since the 1850s, when Oregon poet Joaquin Miller moved here in search of gold. Miller stayed several years with an Indian girl, waxing poetic over the alpine scenery, until an Indian war, and an altercation with a sheriff over a stolen horse, forced him back to Oregon.

"Lonely as God," Miller wrote of the 14,162-foot peak, "and white as a winter moon, Mount Shasta starts up sudden and solitary from the heart of the great black forests of Northern California."

In the late 1800s, Mount Shasta became a favorite retreat of the Scottish-born naturalist John Muir. He spread the mountain's fame with glowing reports of his many climbs, including one harrowing trip when he was trapped overnight on the summit in a subzero blizzard without a sleeping bag. Muir survived only by rolling all night in a sulfurous hot springs puddle.

Since then Mount Shasta has been declared sacred by the Knights of the White Rose, the Rosicrucians, the Association Sananda and Sanat Kimara, the Radiant School of the Seekers and Servers, Understanding Inc., and the I Am Foundation.

This latter group was founded by a Chicago paperhanger, Guy W. Ballard, who claimed to have met a Lemurian named St. Germain high on the mountain's slopes in 1930. The Lemurians, Ballard learned, live in tunnels inside Mount Shasta, but are actually refugees from the ancient kingdom of Mu, now submerged beneath the Pacific Ocean. Like all Lemurians, St. Germain had a walnut-sized sense organ in the middle of this forehead. He also was "clad in jeweled robes, eyes sparkling with light and love."

Other moderns believe Mount Shasta is inhabited by the Secret Commonwealth, concealing the cities of Iletheleme and Yaktayvia in vast caves. The Yaktayvians are said to use the supersonic vibrations from special huge bells to hollow out caves, provide heat, and make light. Intruders are frightened away with high-pitched chimes.

When Janell and I reached our Mount Shasta backpacking destination, South Gate Meadows, we found a lovely heather meadow with a brook tumbling amid wildflowers. We also found that the rocks on the valley floor had been arranged into countless prayer circles. The branches of the few struggling trees at timberline were festooned with spiderweb-like dream catchers woven from brightly colored yarn.

South Gate Meadows is a good day hike goal.

A disgruntled-looking Forest Service ranger was picking up colored ribbons from a former campsite.

"This seems to be a spiritual vortex for a lot of people," I said.

The ranger nodded grimly. "Some of them forget to leave no trace."

That night Janell set her digital camera on a rock outside our tent. She left the shutter open for several minutes to take a picture of star-streaks wheeling around the dark summit of the mountain

Lens-shaped clouds add to Shasta's aura.

above us. While she was busy elsewhere I sneaked into the edge of the picture, holding a flashlight at my chin.

When we looked at the picture later in the tent we both laughed. The spirit of the mountain was there, ghost-like among the shadows.

Eight months later I returned to see Mount Shasta's moods in winter. Janell doesn't care for winter camping, so I went with a couple of Eugene ski chums instead.

In winter the Everitt Memorial Highway is plowed from the city of Mount Shasta for 11 miles to a sno-park at Bunny Flat. This is the usual starting point for mountain climbers headed for the summit. But our goal was different—to ski part-way around the mountain, set up camp, and explore the wilderness at timberline for three days on skis.

The weather did not cooperate. We slogged into the teeth of a blizzard with our heavy backpacks, wearily breaking trail through heavy, crusted snow. After five hours we had managed to ski only 4 miles, and daylight was fading. In a gusty whiteout, somewhere in the wilderness, we tramped a flat spot for the tent and set it up. We anchored it with every snow peg and guy wire we could find in our packs.

That night, as the wind howled across the slopes, shuddering the tent and blasting snow against the fly, it was easy to believe Mount Shasta does have a spirit—an angry spirit telling us, "Go away!"

Winds and avalanches limit winter visits.

The irony was that the very next day, after packing up in hurricane winds and skiing out through a white-line landscape of snow and cloud— the very next day, after driving down from the storm into the sunshine, we looked back at the great white mountain against patches of blue, and I felt I could hear Mount Shasta's voice clearly saying, "Come back!"

Such is Mount Shasta.

58

YOSEMITE FOR
OREGONIANS

R ain? I thought, amazed. "You think it rained in Yosemite Valley today?"

The California-blond ranger nodded glumly. "Nobody shows up in this weather. All the trails are empty."

I realized at once that winter is the right season for Oregonians to visit California's famous national park.

Webfeet obviously have a different idea about what constitutes rain.

OK, so maybe there was a lightning storm in the night, with thunder echoing back and forth from the canyon's granite walls. And yes, perhaps it did drizzle for half an hour at breakfast. But there were also *eight hours* of sunbreaks. I didn't need a coat or an umbrella all day.

February in Yosemite has weather that Oregonians would be happy to see in June.

So here's an off-season guide to Yosemite Valley, when the waterfalls rumble like organ pipes and the wisps of fog seem to have been draped along the cliffs by Ansel Adams himself.

Snow closes the park's high country until July, but Yosemite Valley is so low, at an elevation of just 4000 feet, that it's hikable all year.

If you drive, it's nice to break up the trip with a halfway stop at Mt. Shasta. Four hours south of Eugene on Interstate 5, take the central Mt. Shasta exit, drive a mile east through town, and curve left for 11 miles on the Everitt Memorial Highway to a plowed Sno-Park at timberline with stunning views of the 14,162-foot volcano.

For the night, try the Mount Shasta Ranch (*www.stayinshasta.com*), a bed & breakfast inn at the gabled 1923 mansion of a horse ranch, with a mountain view from the big porch.

Then drive another four hours south on I-5 to Tracy, just south of Stockton. Turn left through Manteca and Oakdale on Highway 120 for two hours to Yosemite Valley. This route takes you through Groveland, an 1849 Gold Rush hamlet with antique stores and saloons. Expect to pay a $20-per-car fee at the national park entrance.

Car traffic in Yosemite Valley is so congested in summer that the valley's road system has been turned into a one-way loop, with a free shuttle bus running every half hour.

Traffic's no problem in winter, but the free shuttle buses are still running, and they're great. They make 21 stops, visiting all the major sights, campgrounds, and trailheads from 7am until 7pm.

Where you stay depends on your budget and your tastes. You don't even need a reservation to stay at Camp 4, a walk-in campground at the Upper Yosemite Falls trailhead where tent sites cost less than $10.

Opposite: Bridal Veil Falls heralds the entrance to Yosemite Valley.

*Half Dome from Mirror Lake.
Below right: Vernal Falls.*

The next step up is Curry Village, with tent-roofed cabins that run a little more than $100 a night. Real cabins are closer to $150. Elegant motel rooms in Yosemite Lodge aren't that much more. Five-star accommodations at the 1927 Ahwahnee Hotel cost up to $500 a night. Reservations at these places are essential (check *www.yosemitepark.com*), but it's easy to get a spot in the off-season.

Wherever you stay you'll be greeted with frantic signs warning you to lock up all food to prevent break-ins by black bears. Campgrounds and trailheads in the valley have been outfitted with 2000 bear-proof metal storage boxes.

The entire park has only about 400 bears. When one of them rips open a car door in search of food, the animal is usually doomed to be relocated or euthanized. To protect the bears, rangers advise that cars left at trailheads with any kind of food (even a half-finished coffee drink) will be towed.

In winter you can't rent horses or bikes in the valley, so hiking's the thing. Here are the top day trips:

Yosemite Falls

Rangers claim this 2,425-foot drop is the world's fifth tallest waterfall in the world, but that height includes a quarter mile of whitewater between Yosemite's upper and lower falls. Certainly one of the most popular trails in the world is the paved 0.2-mile path to the base of Lower Yosemite Falls from Yosemite Lodge at shuttle bus stop 6. Continue past the viewpoint bridge for a 1-mile loop.

Upper Yosemite Falls

Want to see this giant waterfall up close? Start at Camp 4 (shuttle bus stop 7) and switchback up 1000 feet in a mile to Columbia Rock, a viewpoint over-

looking Yosemite Valley. Then continue half a mile to the misty base of Upper Yosemite Falls.

Valley Floor

Part of Yosemite Valley's charm is that sheer granite cliffs rise from an eerily flat valley floor. The Ice Age glaciers that carved the cliffs left a 6-mile-long lake. Now filled with sediment, the former lakebed is home to meadows, oaks, and the meandering Merced River. Trails and paved bike paths along the river make possible many easy loops.

Mirror Lake

Overused and overrated, the 1-mile trail to Mirror Lake follows an old road to a pond that once had a dramatic reflection of Half Dome. The former lake has filled with flood debris and is sprouting a brush forest. The high water of winter is your only chance for a reflection.

Vernal and Nevada Falls

If you set out on the John Muir Trail (from shuttle bus stop 6, be-

The Yosemite Falls Trail.

hind Curry Village) you'll gain 1500 feet in 1.9 miles to a viewpoint of the Merced River's tortuous upper canyon. Turn downhill to the left for 0.3 mile to a footbridge between two of Yosemite's most famous cascades. Here the river slides down a silvery granite slope into Emerald Pool, at the lip of Vernal Falls.

In summer this beautiful spot is packed with tourists and horse tours. In winter, the threat of rain limits your company to Oregonians—and a few dazed foreigners in bright yellow slickers.

But what if it really does rain when you're in Yosemite Valley? Just take the shuttle bus to Yosemite Village. There you can easily spend a day touring the Yosemite Museum, Indian Village, and Ansel Adams Gallery.

Even a Webfoot knows when to come in out of the rain.

59

VOLCANO
IN A
SUNNY SEA

I f you've ever wondered what the eruptions looked like that created the cinder cones and lava flows near the Three Sisters, take a hike on Italy's Stromboli.

This tiny Mediterranean island has one of the world's most active volcanoes. It erupts every four to twelve minutes, spewing clouds of steam by day and fountains of glowing cinders by night. A spectacular hiking trail climbs to a crater viewpoint.

The hike is especially interesting now that South Sister appears to be slowly reawakening. Magma rising beneath South Sister has bulged the mountain's southwest flank ten inches in ten years. The geologic record

shows that South Sister is unlikely to blow up like Mt. St. Helens. Instead, we'll probably get a small eruptive display like the ones visible at Stromboli.

Of course it's more complicated to plan a trek to Stromboli than to South Sister.

For one thing, Stromboli's three-mile-long island is accessible only by boat. Even after you've flown to Italy, the boat ride takes an additional four hours. Hydrofoils leave daily from Naples on the mainland and from

Milazzo on Sicily.

Stromboli has no cars, so the ferries are open only to foot passengers. The streets of the island's five tiny villages are so narrow that the largest vehicles are three-wheeled golf carts. Even the police drive through the alleys in golf carts.

The island also lacks major hotels. Ferries arriving at the dock are met by locals who offer to rent out rooms. Fortunately, there are plenty of these quaint vacation lodgings.

The largest village, San Vincenza, is a three-quarter-mile walk up from the ferry landing. Whitewashed stone houses dot the route, surrounded by olive groves, bananas, prickly pears, and Scotch broom.

In San Vincenza you'll find a volcano tour office where you can sign up for a guided tour to the volcano's summit for a moderate fee. Groups of 25 set out with helmets and flashlights at 5pm each day. They climb to the summit at twilight to see the volcanic fireworks and return at 11pm.

If you'd prefer a free, self-guided 6-mile loop hike, simply walk up a lane that starts in the middle of town, beside a pharmacy near the town's impressive church.

This trail passes a cemetery with graves dating from 900 to 1900 AD. Then the path crosses a lava flow that erupted during the Roman era—about the same time that lava flows last erupted at South Sister.

Stromboli, an Italian island with a reliably active volcano, is accessible only by passenger ferry (opposite: a hydrofoil from Naples). A hiking trail (below) climbs to the crater.

San Vincenza, the largest village on Stromboli, has no cars. The police drive golf carts.

After 2 miles you'll reach a cliff on the edge of the Sciara del Fuoco, a rockslide chute that descends from the peak's five active craters to the sea.

The craters are constantly spewing white steam, bluish gas, and puffs of gray smoke. Every few minutes the mountain rumbles like a freight train thundering by on a metal bridge overhead. Rocks blown out of the craters bounce down the mile-long rockslide, launch off the island's black cobble beach as if from a ski jump, and explode into the sea like artillery shells. Daring sailboats tack just beyond the danger zone to watch the spectacle.

A pizzeria at a trailside viewpoint is the best place to watch eruptions in the evening.

Stromboli has been erupting like this for 2000 years. Every few decades the mountain pauses to send a lava flow down the rockslide, creating a tsunami. All of the island's beaches have tsunami warning signs. Still, the mountain's relative predictability has been a boon for tourism.

If you turn uphill along the summit trail, you'll reach a sign at the 1300-foot level announcing that travel beyond this point is permitted only with a guide.

This is obviously good advice, but a surprising number of daredevils trek to the top on their own. Some even bring sleeping bags to camp on the summit for an uneasy night overlooking the crater fires.

For the loop hike, turn downhill along the Sciara del Fuoco, following a trail for a mile down to a safer viewpoint—a pizzeria called L'Osservatorio.

Every four to twelve minutes fiery fountains send cinders hurtling to the sea.

Order a pizza here and wait for the sun to go down. Tables on the terrace are lit only by candles so the volcano's red cinder fountains are easier to watch. Binoculars bring the fireworks up close. And don't forget a flashlight so you can find your way back along the island's alleyways to your room after dark.

Our Central Oregon volcanoes haven't put on a Stromboli display for a thousand years. But mountains like South Sister are still very much alive. New cinder cones are lava flows are inevitable.

For a sneak preview of the show to come, hike to Stromboli.

60

HUT HOPPING IN AUSTRIA

The Neue Regensburger Hut in the Stubai Valley.

Backpacking in Austria's Alps is all about "hut hopping." Instead of carrying tents, backpackers stay in rustic mountain hotels known as huts—in German, "Hütten".

My wife Janell and I sampled this backpacking system along the Stubai High Trail, where the concept of Austrian huts began.

The original alpine hut really was just a hut, a primitive shelter with a dozen straw mattresses. It was built in the Stubai Valley in the 1880s by Franz Senn, a Tyrolean pastor who hoped tourism might lift his remote mountain parish out of poverty.

Since then more than a thousand trailside lodges have been built throughout the Alps. Although the huts are now rustic hotels with showers and restaurants, most are still accessible only by trail. Meanwhile, old-fashioned backpacking with tents has been banned altogether.

Entirely above timberline, the Stubai High Trail visits eight huts on a spectacular 48-mile loop. The tour passes glaciers, blue-green lakes, and wildflower meadows with clanging sheep bells.

The route also scales a dozen rugged mountain passes. Some are so steep that cables and metal steps have been anchored in the rock to aid hikers. Maps are available at *www.stubaier-hoehenweg.at*.

Few people complete the demanding 48-mile loop in less than eight days. Short on time, Janell and I opted for a smaller loop to five huts in six days.

Starting point for most visitors is the airport in Innsbruck, the scenic capital of Austria's province of Tyrol. Buses leave downtown every hour for the 20-mile trip south to Neustift in the Stubai Valley.

Tourism truly has brought affluence here. Neustift is packed with four-star hotels masquerading as chalets, their geranium-bedecked balconies shaded by huge sloping eaves.

The cheapest bunks are dormitory style.

Our plan was to catch a shuttle van to a trailhead near the first hut, trimming 2000 feet of elevation gain from our first day's hike. We missed the 9:30am van, and learned that a taxi to the same trailhead costs $50. Ouch.

The taxi driver, a local woman in her 40s, told us the Stubai Valley has a permanent population of just 10,000, but hosts 700,000 overnight stays each summer — and 1.2 million during the winter ski season.

She sighed, recalling a less hectic era. As a girl, she had to sleep in the garage each summer because her parents rented her room to guests. Families would hang out a banner that read "Zimmer frei" (room available). Then Mom would cook for the tourists while the kids helped out by peeling potatoes.

Red-white markers and signs show the way.

At the trailhead Janell and I set out with light day packs. The huts have mattresses and blankets, so all you need for the night is a sleep sack — a sheet sewn into the shape of a sleeping bag.

Two miles of climbing brought us to the Franz Senn Hut, a stone hotel perched on a rocky lip atop a waterfall. Supplies sail up to huts like this on aerial cablecars. The cars are generally sturdy enough for beer kegs, but not people.

Many of the sheep have clanging bells.

The Franz Senn Hut is huge, with bunks for 185, but in July and August it's a good idea to call ahead for a reservation. Latecomers end up sleeping on the floor. You won't need reservations for the rest of your tour, however. Once you've started the loop, each hut's host telephones ahead to the next to save you a spot.

Most huts are owned by alpine clubs that regulate prices. A bunk in a semi-private room with two to eight people costs about $30. Bunks run $20 in the hut's "lager" (dormitory), but then you'll share the room with 16 to 30 trekkers, some of them certain to snore.

Bunks are about half price if you're a member of one of the alpine clubs, so it can pay to join. Information is available at *www.alpenverein.de* or *www.alpenverein.at*.

Cooking your own food is discouraged and often prohibited at huts—another reason your pack is so light in Austria. Expect to pay about $12 for a basic hut dinner of dumplings or wurst with sauerkraut. In some huts, competition has brought culinary novelties such as salad bars. Everywhere, mugs of draft beer add to evening cheer.

Breakfast is early! At the Franz Senn Hut, everyone was up by 6:15am. The staff wouldn't even serve sleepyheads who showed up in the dining room after 7:30. By 8:30 the hut was empty, and we were on the trail again.

Europe is so crowded that hiking is a social experience. More than 200 million people live within a day's drive of these mountains.

We got to know several of the 80 hikers heading from the Franz Senn Hut to the next hut. The most puzzling of these was a lone, elderly man who never spoke. We passed him half a dozen times at rest stops and mountain passes. I greeted him with all the various alpine hails: "Servus" (the Austrian greeting), "Grüss Gott" (Bavarian), "Gritzi" (Swiss), and "Hallo" (popular among European kids).

He never responded. We began secretly calling him the "silent man."

That night we stayed at the Neue Regensburger Hut, a smaller lodge with wood beam ceilings and a folksy ambiance. Everyone went by first names, which is rare in Europe but common in remote huts.

At dinner that night we ended up at a table with the silent man. He ordered sauerbraten. A young couple who shared our table ordered dumplings in English. Were they Italian? Russian? After a silent dinner, we all stayed at the table, facing hours of evening boredom.

Janell finally broke the ice.

Soon I was talking to the silent man, a high school English teacher from Bremen in northern Germany. His wife was no longer able to join him on hikes, so he spent his vacations hiking alone.

Janell discovered that the young couple at our table were Poles from Wroclaw (Breslau). The woman worked for Hewlett-Packard in Poland as a translator of English and Dutch. She had chosen this alpine destination from an Internet search. Her husband had driven eight hours here to fulfill her wish. They complained that both of their sets of parents would not fly, would not let them fly, insisted that they live within 50 kilometers of their birthplace, wished they would telephone more often, and wanted to know when they would produce grandchildren.

The next day was the hardest of our tour. We had to kick steps into steep snowfields to cross two high, rugged mountain passes. Trail distances in the Alps are given in hours. A sign said the day's hike was six hours, but that's pure walking time, with no breaks. It took us eight.

The Dresdener Hut, at the end of this exhausting third day, stands at the foot of a huge glacier, but was the tamest alpine hotel we'd seen. The adjacent glacier had been converted into ski runs for a giant resort in 1973. Now gondolas ferry winter skiers and summer hikers up from the highway. Most of the guests at this 160-bed hotel had hiked only 100 yards.

Tirol prohibited the conversion of additional glaciers into ski areas in 1975, so when global warming began crippling ski resorts throughout the Alps in the 1990s, the Stubai resort's glacial ice allowed it to thrive. Even here, the resort covers miles of snowfields with white plastic in summer to slow the melting. Snow machines run all winter. Austrian ski resorts are expected to shutter entirely within 60 years due to lack of snow.

Alpine glaciers are retreating and melting.

The next morning we crossed a short, steep pass to our fourth lodge, the Sulzenau Hut. Only the foundations remain of the original hotel built here in 1926. It was destroyed by an avalanche

The ibex eats alpine lichens.

in 1975. The new hut is concrete, shaped like a giant wedge facing uphill to deflect future slides.

Our table partner that night was yet another of these solitary but tough, fit, elderly men that you meet so often in the Alps. Far from silent, this one was a Munich screenplay writer who had filmed documentaries in Africa, Alaska, and Australia. He told us he was still under an aboriginal death sentence for witnessing forbidden ceremonies. We exchanged addresses and promised to keep in touch.

Although alpine clubs own most huts, they usually hire a family to run the hut as concessionaires. For four generations, the same family has operated the Sulzenau Hut. They pride themselves on ecological management. A small hydro plant generates the hut's electricity. Solar panels provide hot water. All the food is grown locally in the Stubai Valley, and table scraps are fed to pigs in a sty behind the hut.

On our fifth day we crossed a pass where ibexes—wild mountain goats with curving, 3-foot-long horns—were nibbling lichen from granite cliffs. Our final lodge, the Nürnberger Hut, clung to a hillside. Built in 1906 with stone walls, a dormered roof, and red-and-white striped shutters, it surprised us by offering free showers. We hand washed our clothes and hung them to dry in a basement furnace room. At least we would have clean clothes for the final day's hike down to the bus stop at Neustift.

The Alps' most famous hiker, Ötzi, was found in a melting ice field west of the Stubai High Trail in 1991. First aid teams rushed the shriveled corpse by helicopter and then ambulance to an Innsbruck hospital. There they learned that Ötzi had been dead for 5300 years.

The surprisingly well-preserved Copper Age mummy is now displayed in a museum in Bolzano, an hour's drive south in Italy. If you're hut hopping in Austria, it's worth a stop to pay your respects.

As school classes file past the display window inside Ötzi's museum, some of the children squirm and look away. Others gape. Bony and shrunken, the ice man's hand is clenched into a claw. He died with a stone-dagger in his hand, the victim of an arrow wound.

Scientific controversy rages about why Ötzi was hiking so high in the Alps, and how he got into trouble.

Personally, I think he was simply headed to Austria too soon, five millennia before hut hopping became the civilized way to trek the Stubai High Trail.

Plan to eat in the hut's dining room because backpacking stoves are often banned.

A pond reflects peaks at the head of the Stubai Valley near the Dresdner Hut.

61

TURTLING ON THE GREAT BARRIER REEF

There are many reasons to go snorkeling on Australia's Great Barrier Reef, but the impetus for me was my grand-turtle, Luigi.

How many parents have inherited a pet when their children left home?

Hamsters and bunnies have a limited enough lifespan that they don't anchor you forever.

But beware when your daughter buys a tortoise.

In fairness, I should say that my daughter, Karen, was already a college student at the time. She wasn't allowed to have pets in the room she rented. She persuaded her landlady that turtles could not bark at mailmen or climb curtains.

The Hermann's tortoise that Karen purchased was no bigger than an Oreo cookie. Native to the arid hills of Greece, but now bred in captivity, this species routinely lives to be eighty years old, slowly growing until it is the size of a dinner plate.

Such a pet can easily outlive its first owner—and sometimes its second or third. It is possible that some turtles have no natural age limit.

After Karen graduated she accepted a position teaching linguistics at the University of Queensland in Brisbane, Australia.

You can't bring reptiles into Australia. The continent is already crawling with them, and the Aussies don't want to add strange new kinds.

So we were left with custody of the "grand-turtle." Meanwhile Karen, wracked by turtle deprivation, convinced us to come see even bigger turtles on Australia's coral reefs.

The Great Barrier Reef is the largest organic structure on the planet, covering an area larger than the entire state of Oregon.

Tourism is a billion-dollar industry here. Most snorkelers and scuba divers are shuttled out from the Australian mainland for day trips. Although the vast reef system includes some 900 islands, only a few have overnight facilities.

Determined to stay long enough to view the turtles properly, we booked four nights at a frighteningly expensive resort on Heron Island, a quarter-mile-long coral sand cay at the southernmost end of the Great Barrier Reef, exactly on the Tropic of Capricorn.

The 14-hour flight across the Pacific to Sydney was not as horrible as I had anticipated, but it was followed by a one-hour connecting flight north to Brisbane, and an additional one-hour flight farther north to Gladstone, a small steamy coal-shipping port with a dozen giant Chinese freighters anchored offshore.

From Gladstone a three-story catamaran ferry took us two hours out into the choppy Pacific to Heron Island. The ferry docks at a small harbor

The catamaran ferry to Heron Island docks by a wreck used as a breakwater.
Opposite: Karen goes reef walking to explore the sandy reef surrounding the island.

Snorkeling on the reef.

dynamited out of the reef.

The resort on Heron Island began as a turtle soup canning plant in the 1920s, but after three years with little profit, it was sold to a Danish captain who converted it to a sportfishing getaway. When Australia created a national park here, the resort metamorphosed into an upscale ecotourism destination.

Heron Island is so small that you can walk all the way around it in 90 minutes. Tens of thousands of rails, terns, and shearwaters nest in the bushes and trees, squawking and flying everywhere.

As you walk along the beach you'll also notice dark shapes slowly moving through the emerald water. These are green sea turtles and loggerhead turtles. Many of them measure three feet in diameter and weigh a thousand pounds. Hundreds come here between October and March, sometimes swimming thousands of miles to nest on the beach where they were born.

The giant clams have brightly colored lips.

The female turtles wait for a high tide at night. Then they lumber up the beach, dig a three-foot-deep hole in the sand, lay about 120 rubbery ping-pong-ball-sized eggs, cover them up, and lumber back. Turtles between the ages of 35 and 95 may do this up to ten times a summer.

After dinner we watched a green sea turtle dig for an hour and a half, and then lay eggs until midnight. Rangers enforce rules about shading flashlights and keeping your distance, so as not to interfere.

On the way back to our room we found dozens of turtle tracks—sandy

A green sea turtle resting near our patio.

toboggan runs crossing the dark beach. One weary giant, still dragging herself back to the sea, turned to us and sighed.

The next morning, with the turtle excitement temporarily over, we donned our snorkel gear, flopped down to the beach in swim fins, and set out into the lukewarm water.

The Great Barrier Reef is actually a system of nearly 3000 individual reef platforms separated by open ocean. The five-mile-wide reef encircling Heron Island is fairly typical of these platforms, rising about 200 feet above the surrounding seafloor.

Breakers ring the outer edges of the coral plateau, where the reef is slowly growing outward. On the plateau itself, coral grows in clumps in a sandy-bottomed, shallow green lagoon.

Turtle tracks on the beach.

Like a giant tidepool, the reef plateau merges with the ocean at high tide, then drains at low tide until the coral is just barely covered. Coral that grows too tall dies.

When you snorkel at high tide the coral is just out of reach below you. Perhaps the most common type of coral, staghorn coral, has pointy branches that can scrape your swim fins. Staghorn grows fast—as much as a foot a year—but it's also fragile. Cyclones smash its tips to rubble. The resulting debris and sand helps build the plateau.

Brightly colored fish dart among the coral branches. Zucchini-sized sea slugs filter the sand between coral clumps for nutrients. Four-foot-long leopard sharks swim by.

Sharks? Although resort staffers assured us that man-eating varieties don't visit this part of the reef, a shark sighting is still enough to make your snorkel choke.

Heron Island is only a quarter mile wide.

At low tide, reef walkers can explore the lagoon for miles.

Scuba diving is the best way to explore the depths at the edge of the reef plateau, where bigger fish roam, but even if you don't have scuba certification, you can see a lot while snorkeling and reef walking.

Reef walkers set out at low tide, when the lagoon's waters are about knee deep. Walking on the coral itself would be damaging and dangerous, so it's banned. Instead you follow the labyrinth of sandy openings between coral clumps.

The resort provides reef walking equipment at no extra charge. All you need are old tennis shoes, a walking stick, and a glass-bottomed tube that lets you peer underwater.

Outfitted for reef walking, we ambled a mile away from the island, marveling at bright blue starfish and giant purple-lipped clams.

As the tidewater began to rise to our thighs, we realized it was time to hurry back.

Halfway to the beach we spooked a stingray hidden in the sand. It flapped in a lazy circle and faced us, blocking our path again.

Immediately I thought of Steve Irwin, the "Crocodile Hunter" of television fame, who died on the Great Barrier Reef in 2006 when a stingray

OREGON FAVORITES

stabbed a poisonous barb into his chest.

Irwin's widow Terri grew up in Eugene. She still runs the Australian Zoo in Queensland. In his memory she has funded oceanographic research in both Australia and Oregon.

Researchers insist that stingrays don't want to kill you. It takes them six months to replace their venom, so they strike only when threatened.

Luigi considers a Heron Island brochure.

As we sidled past the ray it jerked its tail up in a feint. We bolted for the beach like madmen.

Our last night on Heron Island I woke up at 2am to a strange scraping noise. It sounded as if someone were dragging a wheelless Volkswagen chassis across a driveway, one inch at a time.

I crept to the sliding glass door and pulled the curtain aside.

A giant tortoise was slowly dragging herself across our sandy patio, ramming garden furniture aside as she went.

"Karen!" I whispered loudly. "Come look."

My daughter shambled up sleepily in her pajamas. She looked at the thousand-pound reptile and rubbed her eyes. "Wow. In a few hundred years, that could be Luigi."

As I said, beware when you inherit a grand-turtle.

The stingrays that lurk in the sandy shallows are deadly, but try to avoid trouble.

62

AIMING FOR THE STARS

I an Sullivan was so nervous his fingers were shaking.

With the countdown set to start at 2:50am on New Mexico's White Sands Missile Range, the 26-year-old from Eugene was rechecking the launch time yet again on his laptop computer. His somber look suggested that the young man's career was riding on that night's rocket.

And now I have to confess it is hard for me to give an unemotional report of this particular launch.

You see, I am Ian's father.

Yes, I usually write outdoor columns and hiking guidebooks. But that's not the only reason I'm hesitant to write about Ian.

I don't want to be accused of the boastful dad routine, boring people with the story that my son is a rocket scientist. For most people, "rocket science" means braininess, fame, and glamour.

That's not entirely accurate. Sure, Ian got good grades at South Eugene High School and the University of Oregon. He went on to earn a Ph.D. at Caltech in Pasadena.

But from what I've seen, the life of an actual astrophysicist is marked largely by tedium, stress, hard work, and often failure. A fire-fighter, a doctor, or a teacher would have a better shot at fame or glamour.

Part of the problem is that physics research is hard to explain, especially for a guy like me who writes articles about hiking.

Ian's project goes by the name of CIBER, which stands for the Cosmic Infrared Background ExpeRiment. A dozen scientists in four countries had been working on it for four years under Dr. James Bock, Ian's forty-ish, workaholic advisor at Caltech.

But no one had spent as much time on CIBER as Ian.

As I understand it, CIBER's goal is to fire an infrared telescope into space just long enough to take pictures of the background radiation remaining from the universe's first stars.

Apparently physicists theorize that the Big Bang dispersed matter so thoroughly that 400 million years passed before things coalesced enough for stars to form. Those first suns flared to life with a vengeance, creating a mighty blaze that might still echo faintly as infrared light 13 billion years later.

Ian checks the rocket's telescopes.
Opposite: Liftoff at the White Sands base in New Mexico (NASA photos).

If you could take a picture of that infrared signal you might prove the theory of the Big Bang. Certainly you would learn a lot about how the universe began.

The stakes for this research are high.

Unfortunately, telescopes on the ground can't discern infrared signals from space very well because the Earth's atmosphere is awash with its own infrared light, drowning out other sources.

Orbiting telescopes like the Hubble and the Spitzer are in a much better position to take infrared pictures, but they don't have the right kind of wide-angle camera for the job.

Teams of scientists around the world have been racing to solve this problem. The largest project, the James Webb Space Telescope, is spending billions of dollars to put the perfect infrared camera into orbit.

Ian's CIBER project is a dark horse in this race. CIBER's budget was a mere $1.2 million for the telescope payload, plus a million or so for the NASA rocket.

If CIBER works, it could scoop the James Webb team at less than a

The 15-foot payload.

thousandth of the cost.

But will it work?

On CIBER's original launch date, the infrared camera failed. The camera shutter that Ian built broke at the last minute. That launch was scrubbed just before the final countdown, with the missile standing by.

Humiliated, Ian had to drive back to Caltech from New Mexico with a van full of sullen colleagues and broken equipment.

To this day, Ian has trouble talking about how much that failure hurt. In all honesty, I think he almost gave up on astrophysics. I also believe it was the support of his wife Guinevere Saenger, herself a graduate student of piano, that turned him around.

Ian went back to his lab and redesigned the cursed shutter from scratch, stress-testing every part for failure along the way.

Fast-forward to 2:50am on Wednesday, February 25. The final countdown has begun. Forty minutes to liftoff.

My wife Janell and I have made a long and stressful voyage of our own to attend this launch. When the date was finalized two days before the launch, we boarded a flight from rainy Eugene to sunny El Paso, rented a car, and drove an hour to the hotel in Las Cruces, New Mexico where Ian was staying.

The next day we drove another 45 minutes through the desert to the missile base where Ian had been assembling the rocket payload for a month.

As a guidebook author, I can tell you that White Sands' 100-mile-long valley is too desolate even for sagebrush. Unexploded bomblets from past missile tests make hiking impractical.

On one side of the valley, incessant winds have whipped gypsum dust from a dry lakebed into the scenic white dunes of a national monument.

On the other side of the valley, near the launch site, a surprising variety of wildlife seems to tolerate the harsh environment. Roadrunners, wily coyotes, jackrabbits, and even oryx (antelope introduced from Africa) eke out a living among yucca and mesquite brush.

White Sands is the valley where the world's first atomic bomb exploded in July of 1945. America's space program began here after World War II when captured Nazi scientists helped build and fly V-2 rockets.

Today, security is still so tight that the foreign scientists on Ian's team—even the Canadian—are allowed on base only with a military escort. Cameras are taboo. Military police checked the underside of our car with mirrors.

Janell and I have not even been allowed to see the rocket itself up close. Instead, Ian took us to the empty six-story hangar where it had been assembled.

With pictures and spare parts as show-and-tell props, Ian explained that Black Brant rockets for research projects like this are about 60 feet tall and 18 inches in diameter, with two propulsion stages. The 15-foot payload section includes guidance systems, radio transmitters, a re-entry parachute, and the 3-foot-long CIBER telescope.

The entire flight will last just 15 minutes. Still, that's enough time for the rocket to zoom 220 miles straight up and linger for six minutes of infrared photography. Then the payload lands about 40 miles to the north, where Ian is supposed to fetch it by helicopter at dawn.

If all goes well.

Ten minutes and counting. Ian is in a control bunker 100 feet from the launch site, behind triple-pane glass windows three inches thick.

Janell and I, along with Ian's wife Guinevere, have had to join a cluster of visitors in an observation building half a mile away. On a TV monitor we watch as a metal hangar slides away and the rocket launcher slowly tilts upright.

"Wait!" A woman in combat fatigues suddenly tell us, "We have a delay."

Janell and I look at each other with foreboding. Not again.

"How much of a delay?" I ask.

An Army helicopter takes Ian across the White Sands Desert to the rocket (NASA photos).

"Fifteen minutes."

The added minutes are the slowest of all.

Finally, at 3:45am, a ball of light the size of my thumbnail rises across the dark desert, as swift and silent as a white-hot bullet. The roar arrives a few seconds later. Then the light sputters and the booster rocket falls away. A moment later another, smaller ball of light soars into the stars, directly overhead.

After less than 40 seconds the light blinks out altogether. The second stage has dropped away, leaving the unseen payload to arc into space on its own.

Everyone cheers, but we are also worried. Did the camera shutter open? Will the telescope send back pictures?

The rocket seems to have functioned, but what about Ian's experiment?

Half an hour later we were allowed to drive to the control bunker at the launch site. Strange smoke still hung in the air.

Ian walked up to meet us, his face set in stone.

His wife wrapped her arms around him. "Oh, Ian."

"It's OK," he said, obviously exhausted by stress and lack of sleep.

"Why is it OK?"

Finally he smiled. "We got the data. The camera shutter worked."

Then the night became a blur of cheers and congratulations.

It was only the next day, after Ian had retrieved the payload in the military helicopter, packed a van for the return trip to Pasadena, and grabbed three hours of sleep, that I dared to ask him the question I'd been holding back.

"So, when will you know about the first stars?"

Ian shrugged. "I'll have to analyze the data first. We wouldn't announce anything until we've published a paper about our findings anyway. At least a year."

"A year?"

My son nodded. "This project is controversial. Some people are going to object to whatever we say about the Big Bang. We've got to have our facts straight."

I returned to Eugene having learned a few lessons about astrophysics. Science can't be rushed. It's not about fame.

But I kept watching for that next paper by Ian Sullivan.

A year later, when Ian graduated from Caltech, I asked again. The CIBER results, he said, were interesting, but they weren't as conclusive as he'd like. So instead he'd decided to tackle the problem from an entirely different angle—using a gigantic radio telescope in the Gibson Desert of Western Australia.

"That sounds pretty remote," I said.

He laughed. "The Gibson Desert makes White Sands look like a tropical resort. Want to come see?"

Count me in.

The Organ Mountains rise from the edge of the White Sands missile base.

INDEX

Jefferson Park in September.

Tree on Heron Island, Australia.

About the Author

William L. Sullivan is the author of a dozen books about Oregon, as well as several novels. A fifth-generation Oregonian, he grew up in Salem, graduated from Cornell University in English, studied at Heidelberg University in Germany, and earned a master's degree in German literature from the University of Oregon.

His journal of a 1000-mile backpacking trek across Oregon, *Listening for Coyote*, was chosen one of the state's top 100 books by the Oregon Cultural Heritage Commission. He has written hundreds of outdoor articles — first for *Eugene Weekly* from 1992 to 2000, and since then for the Eugene *Register-Guard*.

He enjoys backcountry ski trekking, playing the pipe organ, promoting libraries, and reading novels in five languages.

He and his wife Janell Sorensen live in Eugene but move each summer to the log cabin they built by hand on a roadless stretch of river in Oregon's Coast Range — a story told in his memoir, *Cabin Fever*.

An illustrated list of Sullivan's books, speaking engagements, and favorite adventures is available at *www.oregonhiking.com*.